CW00357974

STOP POSTPONING THE REST OF YOUR LIFE

Stop
Postponing
the Rest
of Your Life

Paul Stevens

Ten Speed Press
Berkeley, California

Copyright © 1993 by Paul Stevens. All rights reserved. No part of this book may be reproduced in any form, except for brief reviews, without the written permission of the publisher.

Ten Speed Press
P.O. Box 7123
Berkeley, California 94707

cover design by Fifth Street Design

text design by Victor Ichioka

FIRST TEN SPEED PRESS PRINTING 1993

Library of Congress Cataloging in Publication Data

Stevens, Paul, 1941-
    Stop postponing the rest of your life
    Paul Stevens.
    160 p.   cm.
    Includes bibliographical references
    ISBN 0-89815-518-5
    1. Vocation guidance.   2. Career development.   3. Life skills
    I. Title
HF5381.S773   1993
650.1—dc20   92-23608 CIP

Printed in the United States of America

1 2 3 4 5 — 97 96 95 94 93

▓ CONTENTS ▓

■ INTRODUCTION ■

This book is about making your worklife a more satisfying experience.

Look through the following list. If you can't find one or more needs which match yours, this publication is not for you.

- Sorting out what is really important in my life.

- Finding a better balance between career demands, my family's needs and personal desires.

- Understanding where I really am today.

- Separating my worklife worries so that I can deal with them more effectively one by one.

- Establishing what I can do to be less reliant on my employer for my career progress.

- Deciding what I want my future to be like.

- Enjoying my worklife more.

- Removing personal doubts and uncertainties about my career direction.

- Learning what I really have in worklife skills and capabilities.

- Finding alternative ways to progress and grow personally.

- Increasing my self-confidence in my worklife activities.

- Deciding what lies between where I am now and where I want to be.

- Anticipating the future — not just waiting for events to occur or crises to befall me.

- Identifying and scheduling realistic personal goals.

- Evaluating whether the best course is to seek change in my current job, or whether promotion, a transfer or my resignation or early retirement is needed.

- Establishing myself more firmly in a career.

- Searching for a deeper, clearer purpose in my worklife.

▨ *Have you very carefully thought* ▨ *through what you want to do for the remainder of your working life?*

Perhaps you have a growing feeling that before it is too late you want to establish whether you can and should consider a change in your career. Otherwise, you may continue in the same job but still feel dissatisfied, because you will always wonder if you could have made a change.

Perhaps change is being forced on you because of layoffs or the realization that you are in the wrong job. Instead of trying for any vacancy that is advertised, you will want to make full use of this opportunity to review the situation and establish what you should be doing.

Perhaps you are planning ahead. For example, women with children in their teenage years may want to begin preparing to establish themselves in a second career.

Perhaps your family has grown up and left home, so that financial pressures are less. You are free to consider other careers which may have lower salaries, but are likely to be interesting and rewarding.

Whatever your reasons for reviewing your career, you need to take time to:

- put your situation in perspective and establish exactly what changes you can and should consider;

- understand yourself so that you can identify the career best suited to your aptitudes, interests, personality and values;

- reach decisions based on a systematic analysis of yourself, your situation and the opportunities open to you.

Before identifying an alternative career or confirming that you are already in the appropriate one, you need to gather and analyze a considerable amount of information. To skimp on this task could jeopardize your chances for success.

You need to establish the type of work which would suit you, the level of work for which you should aim and the kind of organization in which you are likely to be satisfied.

You need to know the areas of worklife in which you are most successful. If you don't, you won't make the right choices. Once you know your strongest success areas, you can make self-fulfilling, rather than self-defeating, choices.

Paula Robbins endorses this need for self-exploration in her book, *Successful Midlife Career Change*: "If you don't know who you are, what you can do well, what you like and don't like, and where you want to work, you are not going to be able to find a career that will really satisfy you."

Stop Postponing the Rest of Your Life was first published in 1981. People I meet who have read an earlier edition and those who have written to me to share what happened to them, achieved their level of contentment by making choices. These were based on a thorough examination of where they were at that time, the learning experiences from their past and a realistic evaluation of what directions would be best for them.

To mark its 10th anniversary, *Stop Postponing the Rest of Your Life* has now been revised and substantially extended. The method for arriving at an adequate state of self-knowledge is to examine ourselves thoroughly in a structured and nonthreatening manner. What follows in this special edition will help you carry out this critical task.

PART ONE

Achieving Career Satisfaction

Change

*How easy it is for people to change their lives
And yet how hard.
We say—look what the world has done to me,
It is their fault.
And we say—if only, if only—
We spend our whole lives making excuses and blaming others,
Creating and believing the grand illusion
That what happens to us has nothing to do with us.
How much harder it is
To see how we have very carefully made our lives
Exactly as they are,
That we are the authors of these messy tales
And we alone can change the story
If we will.*

Below the Surface: Reflections on Life and Living
Marjorie Pizer (Pinchgut Press, Sydney)

All the separate achievements in a period of career reassessment combined to produce in me a profound, personal revolution; together they built self-esteem and a sense of direction for my life. I grew, or pushed myself, out of a life pattern of depression, lassitude, and anxiety—my greatest achievement of my life to date.

Name withheld on request

1 - WHAT'S WRONG?

Our attitudes towards our occupations are heavily influenced by conventions, expectations, rules and regulations which make the prospect of work satisfaction appear to be complex and difficult, achievable only by a small minority. Our educators, career advisers, friends and contacts tell us that in order to advance, we must compete with our associates at work and beat them at the promotion game. Very few talk about the importance of our personal happiness, our individual differences in capability to withstand the pressures of the rat race, or the basic human need for self-fulfillment. The assumption is that we should select an occupation, gain a qualification related to it and pursue this line of work for forty years or more until retirement age!

This concept of career is reinforced when we attend parties or speak to relatives. Inevitably the question is asked "How is work?", implying "How much further have you advanced since we last met?" Not how satisfied are you with what you are doing, or whether it is the type of job which allows you to do what you believe you are good at or enjoy doing. Over and over again we are bombarded with the myth that our occupation should follow a logical career path upwards through a succession of levels of responsibility and higher pay. No wonder many feel stressed by this continual barrage of expectation for success and ask themselves: "Is there no alternative? Surely upwards is not the only way to go?"

All organizations, whether public service, private enterprise or defense forces, are shaped like a pyramid in the way authority, responsibility and pay are distributed. Pyramids narrow rapidly, so there are very few positions near and at the top. Because of this form of organization, the odds against you reaching the top are very long, no matter how hard you try.

We are in an age of rapid technological change and also, social scientists tell us, the age of the individual. While many are being forced to change occupations because of layoffs, individuals are showing more and more that the traditional career path, marked by achieving promotion and further promotion, is not satisfactory to them.

Alternatives are available and they all involve some form of change. Thousands are changing — some by haphazard methods, others by detailed study and a planned strategy. A lot is at stake! Not only personal feelings of self-worth but also the quality of relationships with family, friends and colleagues. People who are happy at their work radiate an inner contentment that makes them more pleasant to be with, frequently more interesting to talk to and, in many cases, easier to live with.

This book will help you think through the realities of your own situation, decide what is causing dissatisfaction with your worklife and develop a plan to do something different. Most of the difficulties you will encounter are covered here. Achievement is not easy and seldom fast, but the potential rewards are surely worth every effort. You have only one life and limited time to achieve what you really want to do. Your career transition journey starts each time you set out to redefine your worklife needs and wants.

Our changing expectations from work

Today, our values, beliefs and expectations about work are markedly different from those of past generations. Of the millions of people in jobs, few find employers who meet their personal requirements, and the majority are not motivated to work hard. As a consequence, not only do many withdraw emotional involvement from their work, but they insist upon regular increases in pay and employment benefits to compensate for their lack of job satisfaction. The old incentives, such as having a job, do not motivate as they used to. Industrial disputes, poor quality of output or customer service and demands for shorter working hours are visible proof of this.

The value system of former generations, which no longer suffices for today's employees, had many characteristics. If a woman could afford to stay home and not work at a paid job, she did so. As long as a job provided a man with a reasonable living and some degree of security he would put up with other drawbacks. Money and status were the motivating incentives of most people, who were attached to their jobs, not only by bonds of commitment to their family, but also by loyalty to their employers.

The new values expressed in the world of work today contrast significantly. Work itself has become less important and lifestyle management more important in the pursuit of self-fulfillment. More and more women have turned to paid jobs to help fund this interest in lifestyle management or to pursue careers for their own satisfaction.

Less visible is the refusal of many men and women to subordinate their personalities to the work role, to conform for the sake of it. Employees of this decade are demanding that their individuality be recognized.

With the increasing rate of change in the workplace, jobs disappearing and new ones evolving, it is more important than ever for people to think about their career and employment survival. Having a paid job meets important human needs for income, independence, self-respect and belonging to a group, but today's employees want more: a growth in self-esteem by regular feedback of acknowledgment of efforts; the facility to see that their contribution at work makes sense to others; enough stimulation to avoid boredom; and a knowledge of what the whole organization is doing and accomplishing, not just of the results of the immediate work unit. Above all, there is a demand to have a say in decisions which affect their daily worklife. To achieve this, power has to be delegated honestly and without strings from senior management, an action many employers won't risk.

The old carrot and stick approach — money and success through long service leading to promotional opportunities — is not working as well for employers as it did in the past.

Our lack of contentment at work is not so hard to understand when we consider these changes in expectations. Each of us has to assess carefully whether it is the employment environment which is the cause or the occupation or both. It's easier to search out a different type of employment environment than to change one's occupation. But that's not always the right way to go if we value worklife satisfaction.

Career journeys

Our career journey commences before we leave high school and make the transition to higher education or employment. It involves a complex interplay of sociological and psychological aspects, including family social background, sex role stereotyping, ethnicity, home location, perceived influence of parents, teachers and peers, as well as self-assessment of our scholastic abilities. This analysis is undertaken either consciously or unconsciously at a stage in life when we lack sufficient maturity to analyze these factors by ourselves in a logical, systematic manner.

The career path choice is made, or made for us, often in an environment which infers that it is irrevocable. Our destiny for the next forty years is being ordained, or so it seems to us at the time.

Some will commit to this career path choice in a reasonably rational and purposeful manner. Others will drift into a career, or decide seemingly spontaneously. All will start the journey with little or no awareness that it is but the first of many significant worklife decisions we will make before our career journey ends. During this journey we will make many career transitions, some self-initiated, others as a reaction to expected, unexpected or even nonevents in our lives.

Expected events

The major life events we usually expect to be part of our adult life are starting a first job, marrying or finding a life partner, becoming a parent and grandparent, retiring, and finally, dying. Statistics are regularly gathered and published about these expected events, such as age of marriage, retirement and death.

As we traverse childhood and reach adulthood each of us develops a timetable for these expected events. Because of a host of variables our life in fact may not conform to these expectations. Depending on the variables and our attitudes we adjust, either comfortably or not, to expected events which do not occur on our personal timetable. When we start our first job and begin to learn about life at work we similarly form a vision of where our career may take us and calculate approximately when we will reach certain stages in this career. We will encounter many unexpected events and nonevents which will have a great bearing on our worklife and result in the necessity to make decisions which bring about change in our personal situation.

Unexpected events

Secondary schooling, in my personal experience, focused on preparing me for expected events in my adulthood. Role models of previous students were frequently quoted by my teachers in terms of their successes, but the intimacy of their journey to these successes and the setbacks people experienced were not shared. The quest for high performance in learning and its associated exams was merely extrapolated into the theme that this was the foundation for future achievements. I do not recollect one lesson which encouraged discussion about recovering from disappointments in life's journey. The legacy of this education was one of striving at all times to do one's best and the inference that good results, that were also good for me, would follow. Apparently, all I had to do was work hard and rewards would be experienced.

My naïveté did not last long once I started full-time employment. The memory of my early career setbacks is clear, and even thirty years later I am still a little resentful that I was so ill prepared to accommodate them. This is common to many people, as I know from listening to my clients and reading their biographical writings. In fact, I find it very useful to get them to remember how many setbacks they have experienced and conquered.

The view we take of our degree of career satisfaction is a function of several things. When we accept an appointment with an employer we are prepared to provide our time and talents in return for remuneration and psychological success. In this arrangement there is an expectation of a fair trade. One gives of one's self in an expectation of receiving. In reality, the view we have of the degree of equitable balance of this trade changes over time. It changes because of unexpected events of a desirable and/or undesirable nature. Speedy promotion, lack of promotion; surprise pay increase, marginal pay increase; new learning of a nature enjoyed, no significant change in knowledge level, etc. We try to manage these situations continuously. Every now and then the experience is not comfortable. The unexpected event has changed the nature of the trade between us and our employer to a situation where we regard it as unsatisfactory, debilitating or causing discomforting stress. When this occurs we have the choice either to persevere without initiating any change or to take action to redress the balance of the trade. Many do not detect this situation as an opportunity for choice but depend on their employer to implement a remedy. This is an abdication of personal responsibility and an erroneous view. Employers never state explicitly in their employment offer that they will provide happiness or change our job assignments when we want them to.

Whatever career dilemma we are experiencing today needs to be seen as part of the tapestry of life, not as an isolated unexpected event. By perceiving that the dissatisfaction and confusion currently being experienced over worklife, or the emotional hurt due to a recent negative occurrence at work, is part of a mosaic of the reality of living, we can bear up more readily under the strain of it.

The value of unexpected events in our lives is immense. They influence our character development and how we relate to others. That is not to say that we should put off or even avoid career planning but that we should harness what we have already experienced and learn how to manage setbacks more effectively. Often this planning can be successful in avoiding them. And, of course, not all the unexpected events we have experienced are necessarily of a negative nature or outcome. I write with some fervor that what I first perceived as a negative unexpected event — being fired from my employment as a personnel director twelve years ago — subsequently led to an enthralling and deeply satisfying new way of earning and living.

When a person accepts an employment offer it is rarely anticipated that it will lead to moving from this employer to another. Yet in a survey published in the *Occupational Outlook Quarterly, Summer 1989* and in the *Monthly Labor Review, September 1989*, 8.9% to 12% of the U.S. labor force changes careers every year. In 1986, the most recent year surveyed, more than 5 million people did so voluntarily. The significance of the data raises many questions as to what causes employees to resign and seek alternative employment. What unexpected events occur for so many in the early period of their time with a new employer?

I believe that this degree of restlessness is derivative from low levels of satisfaction in their worklife. It also points to the general level of inability among the population to work out for themselves what actually constitutes job satisfaction so that their choice of occupation and employer could be made thoroughly and so reduce the risks in reemployment to those that are worth taking.

Crises brought about by unexpected events occur all through life. We are continually at the beginning of, in the midst of, or resolving changes caused by them. Some are initiated by us due to changed circumstances, some by employers, some by the actions of others. In worklife, when an unexpected event occurs, it is very easy to sink rapidly into depression. Many behave as if they have no control over life events or their reactions to them. They seem to expect negative events to happen and do not believe they are able to prevent their recurrence; the cause and control is seen to be outside their capacity.

Involuntary loss of employment precipitated for me the most unhappy period of my life. My struggle with shame and unhealthy self-pity, loss of self-esteem and an inability to cope with rejection, however, did evolve into a determined search for methods to help others either prevent such occurrences or recover from them. I vividly recollect feeling angry at the time. Such an abyss of unhappiness was not what I felt I deserved. My feelings of defenselessness appalled me but I seemed unable to change them. I retreated from loved ones, friends and acquaintances. The help of others was needed to restore me after this unexpected event in my career. I have subsequently consoled many other experiencing similar unwelcome emotions. I have provided my companionship and skill to assist their recovery. I now know that a structure for our thinking, support and action is the therapy required. It has felt like a mission to explore, design, test and publish such structures and describe the procedures for recovery.

Nonevents

Most people grow from teenage to adulthood expecting to marry. However, this expectation has changed during the last twenty years for couples and single people alike, Some people are not marrying because of their pursuit of personal autonomy. The expectation of being married changes along the way and prompted one of my clients to comment: "I have very much two things running side by side: this ability to be independent and successful and not worry about marriage and parenthood, and a conditioning from my childhood. These have been continually fighting each other."

The life events that occur "on time" in our expectations do not usually precipitate a crisis or self-questioning about their appropriateness. It is the unanticipated or nonevents that cause problems. For some, the incongruities between expected, unexpected or nonevents represent new freedoms for their worklife actions but for others new uncertainties may cause debilitating stress and confusion about what personal action to take. I have not accumulated sufficient money to retire in my early fifties to a tropical island, nor have I climbed Mount Kilimanjaro in Kenya, taken a year off to wander unhurriedly through other cultures or pursue at leisure my interest in Renaissance literature. Nor have I fathered three children as I and my partner planned following our wedding. I am sure you can recite a similar litany of plans, fantasies, dreams and intentions which have not eventuated. What is important is how each of us accommodates their nonoccurrence. If we dwell too much on what might have been it will reduce our energies and commitment to realizing what is yet to come. It will imperil working out precisely what it is we want to happen and working hard to increase its likelihood. This implies taking stock of how far we have journeyed, auditing who we are today and determining what really matters. Along this life journey we have changed, adjusted, compromised, set new goals a thousand times. What has been lacking in many lives is a reliable structure or method by which to undertake this task and so reduce the incidence of nonevents by turning them into expected events. Shakespeare expressed this so ably in the 16th century:

> There is a history in all men's lives,
> Figuring the nature of the times deceased;
> The which observed, a man may prophesy,
> With a near aim, of the main chance of things,
> As yet not come to life; which in their seeds,
> And weak beginnings, lie intreasured.

Aging and change

Our feelings reflect our own personality at any age. Living in a rapidly changing society such as ours requires flexibility in adjusting to both the social realities external to us and the discernible changes within us. Some people may feel they haven't made it in synchronization with their anticipated event if they're not promoted to managing director by age thirty-five; others may delay parenthood in order to consolidate their career future and feel anguished about this decision. Age consciousness still prevails, but in the context of personal career management we can choose whether we let it be either a stimulus or a brake on our worklife actions.

How we react at different ages to unanticipated and nonevents differs from one to another. My work with my clients indicates that the timing of events in our adult years is so variable that we cannot assume that particular transitions will occur at specific ages, nor that a person's behavior will be consistent when experiencing a similar transition. Throughout adulthood, age is a poor predictor of the timing of events, a person's interests, needs or work status. The nature of the career transition, whether recovering from lost employment, reacting to the change of ownership of an employer or losing out on a coveted promotion depends more on how it alters our role, relationships, routines and assumptions. We cope with the transition according to our reaction to these factors and our resources at the time, such as money, self-confidence, emotional stability, personal philosophy, values and self-view.

Change brings about a reaction within us and we differ over the time period of its effect as to the good or not so good nature of this reaction. Job loss, unsatisfactory relocation and other career setbacks require that, when helping people recover, their resources and weaknesses need to be examined in relation to their own view of strategies. In each of these four areas lies the opportunity to diagnose which needs more attention than the other. By systematically sizing up each of them we can learn how to build on our strengths and reduce the negative effects. Every change event or career setback is an opportunity for personal growth. But many have difficulty in perceiving this and often need help to restore their morale and take steps to accelerate recovery.

You may have to contend with the age problem in deciding on a new career path and achieving the transition. You may appear to be too young or too old when your research into alternatives reveals minimum and maximum entry requirements. Or you will come across that unfortunate aspect of many recruitment practices, the prejudice against age. Many professional associations and far too many employers impose obstacles to the mature-age career path changer. A scan of recruitment advertisements could give one the general impression that the only people wanted are between twenty-five and thirty-five. When reasons are reluctantly given by employers, they range from concerns over employment benefit and insurance plans; outdated knowledge; age mix within the firm and — the most unjust ones of all — expectations of conservatism and poor energy levels! Yet don't all organizations in their unwritten rules require conformity? How can they judge energy levels without a face-to-face interview? Those brief, barely polite rejection letters are received far too frequently by the older job seeker who is not given the opportunity to present their case for further consideration personally.

▨ ***No one can make you feel*** *▨*
the wrong age without your consent.

Our changing society has brought about new social meanings of age and age-appropriate behaviors. Whether implementing a career change or career realignment age, has more to do with the assumed attitudes of current or prospective employers than with the individual. Traditionally, there has been a tendency to segregate people into age groups which undertake activities such as education, parenthood, work and retirement as they journey through a particular age band. These attitudes ignore the real-life situations of people. The 1989 Nobel Prize winner for Literature, Camilo Jose Cela, endorses this reality when commenting: "Man has as many lives as years he's lived, and today I am in my seventy-third life." Just as more people are marrying, divorcing, remarrying through their sixties and seventies, so occupational activity can be altered with realizable opportunities for new worklife experiences.

Career renewal can be initiated at any age. There should be more media exposure of such career behaviors to accompany the portrayals of the Veterans' Olympics and sexagenarian first-time authors. Even pop stars such as Jerry Lee Lewis, Tina Turner and Little Richard are redefining career life cycles by continuing to be successful. Frank Sinatra, Victor Borge and Mel Torme have more competition for the consumers' entertainment dollar.

This blurring of traditional life stages does not mean that employment regulations relating to age are changing at the same pace. The difficulties faced by career renewal in the latter period of life are more inhibited than facilitated by employment law and employers' personnel practices. Yet progress is being made.

Influences of other people

When we individually give meaning to our own life's journey we must also accommodate the needs of others. Sadly, many go too far with the latter and deny themselves opportunities for the renewed growth and satisfaction which is available from the pursuit of meaningful work.

Partnerships and families function as social systems. Members are together for a common purpose. Spoken and unspoken rules govern the interactions between members. Just like other systems, each adjusts to maintain a balance. For example, when money is short, all members cut back on spending. But when a family member is having trouble with their worklife, attempts at stabilizing the balance in relationships are often endangered. Like incidences of severe illness, alcohol or drug problems, at these times there is greater risk of strife between the adult members, sometimes causing separation or even divorce. Where conflict between work and positive attitudes to living exists and is allowed to continue, the social system can easily break down causing, alienation and anguish not only to the member experiencing the worklife difficulties, but to the entire family. This contributes to the barriers preventing clear self-perception by each person.

Expectations of others

Our worklife does have an impact on both our intimate and social relationships. Fear of failure, work performance anxiety, the dynamics of relationships affect more than the person experiencing the career dilemma. The expectations of others feature both negatively and positively in the lives of my clients. Many are living other people's lives. In some cases the dominant influence is from a family member already deceased. In carrying out career analysis as a prelude to career planning it is important to identify to what degree the expectations of others have been absorbed. The quest is who you really are today, what you really want and expect from yourself. As none of us is devoid of memories, childhood experiences, family membership or current relationships, we need to identify who has influences and continues to influence our values and self-concept, and by how much. We need to think about the significant people in our life and what they expect of us in terms of our worklife. What do others want us to be, to do or to think? Once this analysis has been completed it is easier to determine what is our own thinking and what is inherited or absorbed from others, and needs to be identified clearly as such.

Too many people spend too much time endeavoring to please their bosses. Genuine motivation for work can only come from within each person; from the awareness that the nature of the work we do is right for us as a unique, individual person. If this is lacking, no amount of praise or threat from another will make us truly happy or highly productive at work.

Significant other

It is not unusual for a person grappling with a worklife problem to endeavor to disguise their situation from the significant other person in their life. A deteriorating career or work-based situation, even loss of a job, may be covered up by the maintenance of the daily routine. Not only does this usually lead to surprise and conflict at some stage when the discovery is made, but such people have also denied themselves the opportunity to verify their self-understanding with one who knows them well.

Whether residing together or dating regularly, the significant other has to accommodate the changes a person may make when resolving a lack of satisfaction with their worklife. The significant other is likely to be more supportive if allowed to contribute to the analysis of what needs to be done, the subsequent career transition activities and the decision making required at several points along the way. Conversely, some people are in relationships where the significant other is affecting their worklife activities negatively.

The barrier of nonfulfillment

You have acquired good experience and perhaps, a formal qualification related to it, in your current occupation. Your training — the combination of experience and qualifications — is inseparable from your job satisfaction needs. Both depend on your employer's management to unlock your full career potential. Alas, what you have acquired has only increased frustration in your worklife. You might be in a "sunset job" — one which has a set timespan and will cease to exist after a certain period.

Many employees have abandoned their occupations because they have met this barrier of nonfulfillment. It is a sad waste of what has been so often a substantial investment of time and money in a career over several years. The sadder aspect is that many abandon their occupation and withdraw their experience and training from the community as a whole, not just from their current employer.

An engineer said to me recently: "It took the bankruptcy of the company to make me start reassessing my values and ask, What do I really want? I now work at a lower position and the family lives more simply. I used to work twelve hours a day and I couldn't see any alternative. I almost lost my wife, kids and sanity!"

Our job satisfaction needs are easy to express, yet apparently difficult for our employers to provide. Not all of us hanker after responsibility and power. But check carefully that the nonfulfillment barrier is not the only issue, before you rush to resign.

Burnout

If you are in a state of continual fatigue — the sort of fatigue neither ten hours' sleep nor a week's holiday relieves — you could be a victim of worklife burnout. It is often accompanied by feelings of extreme frustration. A dedication to work which is not being met by internal rewards of self-esteem and a lack of external indicators from others that your efforts are appreciated both characterize a state of mind now diagnosed as burnout. You are probably trying harder and harder but accomplishing less and less.

Your emotional self may be depressed, easily disappointed or repeatedly irritable. Your physical symptoms may be fatigue, sleeplessness or recurring headaches. If you have been consistently an achiever in your activities, these symptoms will surprise and concern you. You will probably deny that they exist.

Relentless pursuit of one goal without the balance of other objectives in your life will eventually force you to take "time out" to analyze your condition. If you don't, a friend, relative or work associate is likely to intervene and attempt to make you realize that you have a problem. Such assistance should not be rejected. It could trigger a chain of events which may help you to avoid collapse from physical exhaustion or mental stress, or prevent you from turning to alcohol or drugs.

Self-awareness is the way to a solution. Not casual reflection on how far you have come or what success has brought you, but a process of analysis which uses your past and present to map out a plan for the future. Such a plan should contain much more than work goals and schedules for their accomplishment.

Your self-analysis may well identify a hitherto buried desire for a different way of earning a living and challenge your assumptions about your physical and mental capabilities.

Layoffs

You may be about to lose your job or have already lost it through no fault of your own. It may be through staff reduction due to technological change such as computerization, your company's sales dropping, being relocated, a take-over or merger with another organization. Other reasons may be changes in import tariffs, market changes in product demand or simply your skills becoming obsolete or inadequate for your current job or profession.

Apart from making sure that calculations of your termination entitlements are accurate and stated clearly (preferably in written form), you should consider seeking your terminating employer's financial assistance for:

- a worklife counsellor, experienced in informing people in your position about career guidance and job-searching techniques;

- a financial counsellor to advise on the optimum use of lump sum payments plus help with the composition of a contingency weekly budget plan until alternative employment is secured;

- a medical practitioner, occupational health specialist or psychotherapist to be available to guide you in emotion-management techniques, particularly if your job search becomes extended over a long period.

A recent consultancy assignment I undertook for an employer included, in addition to the above specialists, the assignment of the services of an industrial chaplain to help the ex-employees and their families to cope with their situation.

Reduction or retrenchment can be a traumatic experience. It can also be the event which triggers a desire for a career change, particularly if the demand for your occupation is likely to remain low for some time. The essential aspect is not to dwell on how you were informed or how the separation process was handled but to get on with the task of living. Many people have looked back on such an event as a fortunate experience leading to a more satisfying and rewarding occupation. Make sure you are one of these, rather than risking feelings expressed in a letter I received earlier this year:

> *I have been laid off after twenty years' service. My severance pay and benefits will be nearly $200,000. I should be happy, but I'm full of fear for the future. I understand that there must be grieving for the loss of a job, but the tension is so strong that I fear that I will die. At the moment I can't bear the thought of being alone in the world outside my former employment.*

Unemployment benefits prevent those who lose their jobs from starving. The real suffering is often primarily psychological. Without a job, one can quickly feel degraded and deprived of purpose. Unemployment induces shame and reduces self-respect. Action is what is required to change these feelings; action which may motivate you to try a whole range of worthwhile activities you never previously thought of undertaking. Out of these can emerge a particularly attractive occupation, a renewal of enthusiasm, a different and challenging career.

Many things happen to us during our lives that aren't easy; losing one's job is just one of them. But it needn't be the end of the world. It's an opportunity to sample another part of life, an option to try something new.

The mid-career crisis

If you are between the ages of thirty and fifty your unease could be the effects of a mid-career crisis. Popularly known as a mid-life crisis, it is a period of change, turmoil and disillusionment that most people experience to some degree. It is a significant point in our lives, causing consternation because new problems arise to which there appear to be no immediate answers.

The external symptoms can be increased consumption of alcohol, cigarettes and analgesics. Less visible to others can be insomnia, aches and pains, loneliness and general dissatisfaction with life and career. Increased anxiety about physical appearance is not uncommon.

A chasm appears between personal aspirations and actual achievements in worklife. Rarely does one have access through their employer to confidential counselling or life planning workshops or seminars.

For men there is self-questioning about what they are doing with their lives — a realization that not all their ambitions will be fulfilled. Often this is accompanied by a slowing down of the growth rate in salary and frequency of promotion. The worst feelings are a sense of failure, depression which may fluctuate from day to day and frustration at being locked into an occupation with no apparent escape.

For women, in addition to a sense of futility a major hormonal upheaval may occur affecting both the physical and emotional states.

A home, children and love relationship with spouse are goals already achieved by many in the age group prone to mid-career crisis. The question arises: What can I aim for with the rest of my life? A sense of urgency occurs, almost panic, as we wrestle with conflicting thoughts. It's frequently the period when we question whether our current occupation is really satisfying our need for fulfillment, self-esteem and achievement.

It is a matter of interpretation whether Dante was describing his own mid-career crisis in *The Divine Comedy* when he wrote: "In the middle of the journey of my life, I came to myself with a dark wood where the straight way was lost. Ah, how hard it is to tell of that work savage and harsh and dense. The thought of which renews my fear. So bitter is it that death is hardly more." It is difficult for those experiencing this confusion to accept that the mid-career crisis is an opportunity to move towards a fuller, more satisfying life.

What is often needed at this time is a sympathetic ear and moral support as we try to unravel the confusion. It's critical to diagnose whether or not a change of occupation is really desired. A change of employer or location may be a better alternative.

No one should depend on their employer to provide a continually stimulating and exciting career. The world of work just does not guarantee this. Mid-career crisis sufferers should consider other avenues when lack of self-fulfillment becomes a serious concern. Hobbies abandoned during the earlier career growth phase could be taken up again, enrolling in part-time activities, writing, painting or sports are some examples of alternative activities.

If an alternative career is decided upon, maturity and experience will be an invaluable aid in the research, diagnosis and planning necessary to achieve a successful occupational transition.

A mid-career crisis can leave one strengthened and enriched, or weakened, even ill. Rarely does it leave one unchanged. It's common sense to seek help if confusion or depression persists over several months.

Many emerge from the experience with a stronger personality, renewed energy and inner calmness. Many do change careers and, whether successful or not in material terms, are pleased they have made a second attempt, thus taking a new lease on life.

The route to the truth

Work dissatisfaction is an active process in which we ourselves, rather than our employers, create and maintain attitudes which lead to a sense of annoyance and bitterness and feelings of being trapped.

Those who are currently feeling depressed and emotionally frustrated with their worklife may find this statement difficult to accept, implying as it does that none of us really needs to be unhappy at work or confused about the direction of our career. Yet the truth is that everything we need to know to resolve feelings of dissatisfaction with our current work situation already exists within each of us. Our task is to unearth this information.

To identify more promising career directions or to change occupations with confidence requires no exceptional level of intelligence or education. We can all revise and accelerate our career progress at any time in our lives. It is never too late.

But it does require motivation. You must have a strong urge to improve your worklife situation, and you must guard against the immobilizing beliefs that keep many people tied to unsatisfactory jobs.

It is easy to convince yourself that your work dissatisfaction is either unalterable or can only be changed through some very difficult process. Especially depressing can be thoughts that you are inadequate in some way, or that the route to a happier worklife depends on luck. Or that the actions of others are necessary to transport you magically into an alternative worklife situation in which happiness will be found.

The resolution to put such thoughts aside and make a change occurs in different ways to different people. The method by which we rediscover an enthusiasm for work and find a career suited to our unique characteristics differs greatly from one to another. The process common to all has to be hard work, enthusiasm and a determination to feel more in charge of the direction of our lives.

Scanning the recruitment advertisements and the help wanted ads in newspapers and business journals is not a reliable method of finding job satisfaction. You may pass an enjoyable Saturday afternoon wistfully fantasizing about how you would feel in the enticing job roles the advertisements describe. In fact, they seem to want you very much; you are urged to contact the advertiser quickly. Resist the lure of the professionally written copy and think how unlikely it is that the perfect worklife situation can be identified so easily. Human beings are far too complex for this method to be reliable.

The first step to renewal of career satisfaction must be self-analysis. If you don't find out who you are today, where you have been and where you want to go, any steps you take will be blind and precarious. You need to discover by rational analysis what you like and don't like; where and how you want to work; who you want to please — yourself, your parents, your current boss, your lover, your spouse — just who will actually benefit from sorting out this complex subject?

It is important to analyze your past and build on both the good and not so good, rather than push bad experiences under the carpet. The present is the next stage of analysis. You must find out who you really are today before taking charge of where you will be tomorrow.

Our ability to transcend worklife difficulties and identify new fruitful directions is limitless. Once started, the process inevitably leads to an increase in self-awareness and a revised inner wisdom — in short, it's a personal growth process. We are responsible for everything we do. Managing our careers is part of this responsibility. There are always options available to us any time we are willing to take this responsibility and set out to change things.

Stop postponing the rest of your life

We can spend too much time thinking about the future and dreaming of what our working lives could be. It's human nature to put off the hard work — the planning and researching, deciding on the goal and getting things accomplished. Yet nothing of any real substance is going to happen unless we do. How does one get started? First of all, we have to approach procrastination as an obstacle that, once recognized, becomes easier to deal with. In other words, merely thinking about the ideal occupation allows the imagination to conjure up many feelings about having to confront the issues involved.

You are going to have to sacrifice some of your free time, sit down and do some hard work. How many times have you noticed that once you actually start a project you really enjoy it; you become caught up in the momentum that your effort has produced? Of course there are obstacles, frustrations and annoyances during the project. You may have bought a house, or dismantled and reassembled a motor, or prepared for an overseas trip. Any of these would have involved "stops" and "starts", difficulties and hard work. But the pleasure when the goal is reached makes most of it seem insignificant, even humorous on reflection, when you are enjoying the fruits of your preparation and labor.

Here are some suggestions on how to stop postponing the rest of your life. Overcome the temptation to procrastinate and start working *now* towards a new goal.

- Break down the big job of self-analysis and goal setting into small tasks. From a psychological standpoint, if you are faced with a series of relatively smaller tasks, as opposed to one large one, you are more likely to start sooner. Not only are the smaller tasks less of an obstacle to overcome but you also benefit from the positive feedback as you accomplish each section towards your goal.

- Get things under way enthusiastically. Take regular breaks, go for a little exercise — a short jog, a brisk walk, a swim. Whatever you do, rest for a while afterwards and allow your thoughts to turn back to the project. Get to the point where you can visualize the entire task. You'll discover that when you pick up your pen again you'll have a surge of physical and mental energy that will take you through the difficult parts and the momentum will sustain your enthusiasm.

- Be wary of that momentum, though. Give yourself a chance to breathe. You do need to relax from time to time when sorting out your future life. Plan realistic schedules for each stage. Reward yourself with a treat when a particularly difficult obstacle has been thought through and resolved. This kind of internalized incentive plan is just the kind of stimulus to get you back to work again on the analysis, research and planning activities.

- Don't cloud your thoughts at this stage with concerns of how you are going to find new occupational choices. Reflect on the words of that great storyteller, Ralph Hammond Innes in *The Strode Venturer*:

> *"When you know WHAT you want, the rest follows. Don't just drift into something because it offers security, security is never worth a damn. We are meant to live and to live means living dangerously. Half on the edge of trouble, half on the edge of achievement."*

2- WHAT NEEDS TO BE CONSIDERED?

The career life cycle

I've enjoyed being a nurse. I now want to explore my capabilities in something new.

Each career has a life cycle which has four discrete stages: Exploration, Advancement, Maintenance and Decline. It was not so very long ago that social scientists and career researchers believed that each person traversed each of these stages just once in a working lifetime. Today's common pattern of multiple careers during our adult years proves otherwise. In fact, my observations of the career records of my clients indicate that a person can traverse all stages of the career life cycle in as short a period as eight years. Obviously, this requires people to evaluate, make personal decisions and implement career transition actions at several points during their adulthood.

3 yrs!

The Exploration stage involved making job and/or employer choices, settling down into a routine, growing in familiarity with the tasks of the occupation and making tentative conclusions about whether it appeals. Some choose a career with care, others react to circumstances and "find" themselves within a particular career path.

The Advancement stage usually involves the experience of promotion and an increase in the difficulty of work tasks undertaken. Employees also have to deal with rivalry from coworkers seeking similar goals. Conflicts between career and nonwork time allocation begin to materialize and there is usually a desire to seek changes at work that are considered important.

The Maintenance stage can be a complex and confusing period as people reorganize their thinking about themselves in relation to work, the people they care for and the community. They may be conscious of and apprehensive about perceived competition from colleagues and subordinates for similar jobs or even their own position.

Ambitions require adjustment and this process of thinking can be characterized by loneliness, even when close family relationships exist. Eagerness to implement change becomes less urgent and employees consider the dangers of failure and loss of respect from colleagues before acting on or withdrawing proposals. The main clue to identifying whether the Maintenance stage has been reached is when the new possibilities in our job are no longer as stimulating and of no more than peripheral interest.

The Decline stage beckons if the conclusions from the Maintenance stage are not clear or are ignored. Many realign their career directions and so avoid this stage. Others, aware of considerable inner discord, persevere in familiar job surroundings but are concerned that their waning enthusiasm for this kind of work will be spotted by those who have "power" over their fate. Some people are able to traverse this stage comfortably by making the effort to consolidate their career, not by seeking higher risk positions but by shifting from a power role to one of consultation and guidance to others. Their interest changes to wanting to influence others through a lateral relationship rather than one of a command nature. Others identify, negotiate and implement changes to enrich the content of their job. Without such adjustments, people are in the danger zone of, for example, declining self-esteem, waning performance of job tasks and risking being fired or retrenched. At its worst, psychosomatic symptoms occur such as sleeplessness, increased irritability and sometimes, increased intake of alcohol, pills or tobacco.

A concise way of describing career life cycles is to say that in the beginning we are ambitious and keen to make it to a position of significance. This is followed by trying to maintain the position we have reached. The final phase is when we come to the conclusion that we will choose to do only the things which give us personal satisfaction and that the opinions of others are less important or can even be ignored. Our orientations towards either getting ahead, seeking security, wanting more time for nonwork activities or demanding more freedom in how tasks should be carried out, fluctuate many times during our working lifetime. What we value in our careers does change.

The rate at which people traverse the career life cycle and make career transitions has been escalating in the past decade. It is likely that a teenager leaving school this year will experience five or more distinct career changes before retiring from the work force. Some will not retire, but continue working until they die because they derive satisfaction from the nature of their worklife activities.

Self

I don't feel comfortable with the idea of personal success and opportunities. I have never been encouraged to aim high but to feel protective of others and to see material wealth as a bit immoral and unfair.

Career transitions from one career life cycle to another can test you in many ways. There is hard work in analyzing what you want to do, researching information about the proposed direction and developing and following a plan through to its achievement. Making a worklife change is liable to shake up one's whole life. The possible new satisfactions have to be balanced against problems to be encountered on the way to their achievement. Sometimes analysis of options shows that the latter appear to outweigh the former.

While a career transition is a very personal process it will place you out in the open for critical judgment by friends, acquaintances, examiners and ultimately, those with the authority to employ or promote you in your chosen occupation. Not only will you have to cope with difficulties of adaptation but with the discouraging attitudes, criticisms and resistance of others.

It is likely that your career transition will involve a change in status, altering your income level and potential earnings, and creating the need to justify your decision to yourself and others each step of the way.

On the other hand, trying to ignore or resist the need to change can produce despondency, feelings of being trapped and a deterioration in your mental, and sometimes physical, health and relationships with others.

When looking back over their transition period, many report that despite feelings of hesitancy, a moment occurred when they made up their minds and, with strong determination, set out to alter their worklife. For some it occurred within three months of identifying the cause of their dissatisfaction; for others it took as long as two years. But once resolved, the process, despite the obstacles, was much easier after that moment had occurred. It was seized as the opportunity to make life more acceptable and to take command of one's own destiny rather than surrender to the dictation of events or unappealing employer prerogatives.

Taking on a new career direction or retraining in preparation for the transition can make new physical demands on you. It is common sense to have a thorough medical check-up before embarking upon a changed worklife. A medical condition which is not serious in

guard against frustration - jumping in too quickly different standards of living)

.. is some requirement for justific^n **29** (cf. p.30)

What Needs To Be Considered?

① Merely the act of seriously going thru this book means I've not allowed myself to become entrenched in the comfort zone.

youth may become more so later in life. Physical fitness is important, not only to withstand the increased stresses which will be experienced during the transition, but to avoid any possibility that poor health may threaten an appointment to a new job requiring a pre-employment medical examination.

Strict health standards apply to a number of occupations. Often hearing, height, vision, weight, pulse, breathing rate and blood pressure have to meet certain specifications. Don't neglect to research this aspect of your occupational goal when gathering information on entry requirements.

Risk taking

At thirty-three I am too old to be a whiz kid with promise, yet I lack the experience to be considered a seasoned high flyer.

There is unlikely to be a way to improve your worklife position without taking some risk. Part Two of this book helps you reduce the degree of risk by undertaking a logical and thorough self-assessment leading to identifying what you really want to do. If you conclude, for whatever reason, that any degree of risk is not for you, then that in itself has a clear message — stay where you are and with what you are doing — or find a safer employment environment or set of job tasks with your current employer.

Yet while you ponder this recommendation, do consider the number of years until your retirement date, the incidence of premature death, the forbidding prospect of arriving at retirement age and concluding that most of your worklife has been unsatisfactory and wasted. The choice is yours — no one else can make it for you.

In recent years it has become more acceptable to change occupations and career direction. Diploma and degree level study and continuing education for mature-age students has become much more readily available. These factors create a climate in which individuals are now more prepared to change jobs — and even occupations — in order to fulfill personal needs, whether for more pay, greater challenge or personal convenience. While some choose change, others are propelled into changes through the lack of opportunity for promotion or by the trauma of being sacked. One job for life? Certainly not as a recipe for career satisfaction. Many career experts and consultants recommend varied experience gained by means of planned job changes. Often people are not aware that skills they have developed

Self-employment

Self-employment appeals to many, particularly if they have lost a job and feel bitter towards employers. To be in charge of one's own destiny is the dream of the newly unemployed and the unhappily employed.

Small business has daunting obstacles to success. But the attractions and compensations are considerable. It can provide employment, good fun and financial independence. The freedom of the small business operator enables them to devote time to new projects or ventures, to allocate resources without concern about public shareholders, management rivals or bureaucratic back-stabbing. It can also be seen as freedom from the tyranny of nine-to-five vocational slavery.

Enthusiasm is not the only requisite for success in self-employment. Research, research and more research, plus the courage to take risks, are essential. Minimum capital required will vary according to the nature of service, product and location of the business. Whatever the project's nature there is no known instant recipe for success, otherwise there would be no employees. Each person entering self-employment will need sufficient money to live on for business expenses and family commitments during the early stages. Insufficient savings, rather than lack of hard work, is often the reason small businesses fail.

People who start their own business may have only one area of expertise and are going to need a lot more, covering the skills of marketing, accounting, law, purchasing and advertising.

Reading relevant books, questioning others and common sense are underemphasized aspects of likely success. A wide range of self-help books are available in libraries and bookshops. Government sponsored small business agencies provide a consultancy service for virtually all areas of business including finance, management techniques, marketing, cash flow, pricing, distribution, production, taxation and inventory control. Friends and associates are often reservoirs of useful knowledge and experience.

Don't hesitate to question people already in the same line of business; discuss your true asset and liability position and loan eligibility with the small business adviser at your bank; select a lawyer and accountant on whom you can rely and share personal details and apprehensions. Involve your insurance agent and discuss income protection in the event of your becoming sick or sustaining an accident. Engage other business people in conversation on the area in which you intend to establish yourself. Investigate planned changes in regulations, zoning, etc. with the relevant local council and chamber of commerce. Completing these tasks gives a greater chance of success.

and used in one occupation may be transferred to another. Many alternative career prospects can be revealed by identifying all your skills in detail. In the process, risk taking is reduced to only those that are worth taking.

Work and stress

We are constantly told that stress can kill us or cause serious deterioration in our health. Many employers have stress management programs, gymnasiums on company premises, cardiac units in their occupational health centers and financial subsidies for employees who participate in meditation, psychotherapy or biofeedback techniques. These approaches are palliatives that do not deal with the basic causes of stress — or with why stress is healthy for some people and not for others. The stress message is a negative one: that stress is harmful and attempts to reduce it are essential and that stress should be avoided whenever possible. Little acknowledgment is given to the fact that stress can be a positive feature of our lives.

Most stress messages emphasize inner conflicts as the cause, rather than looking at how we interact with different aspects of our environment — both at work and leisure.

Recent research findings state that stress resides neither in the person nor in the situation alone, but depends on how we appraise and react to particular events. Reaction to stress depends on other factors such as early childhood experiences, physiological predisposition and personality, which contribute to more or less resilience. These opinions seem to be borne out when a person loses a job. Some see it as a catastrophe — an irreplaceable loss indicating unworthiness, the only direction being downward. Others see the event as one which falls within the range of risks accepted when the job was taken. Many view the experience as an opportunity to find a new career better suited to their abilities and interests.

Researchers recommend that we reassess our basic motivations, identify what aspects of employment produce good or bad stress effects on our mental and physical health, and then seek out an occupational environment which is as closely tailored to our individual needs and likely reactions as possible. This is a more logical approach than that of viewing stress as totally bad. It gives us the reassurance that we can control our own situation with the right research.

Some of us are like racehorses and are only happy with a vigorous, fastpaced work environment; others need peace and tranquil surroundings in which to be creative and fulfilled in our worklife.

Many work exceptionally long hours without becoming ill, while others in apparently easier occupations develop ulcers, hypertension or heart disease.

Our health, ability to continue earning, relationships with others, as well as our personal happiness, are all at stake in this frenzied, trauma-filled world. The decision to allocate some time to carry out a thorough review of our worklife situation and identify those occupational factors which are most likely to enable us to perform well, free from the negative aspects of stress, is clearly a vital one.

Promotion

I am not interested in the struggle for ascendancy which involves good ideas being cast aside because someone feels threatened, or because the current fashion is to do it differently.

In most jobs, the way to obtain higher pay, status or authority is to earn promotion to management levels. But the work of a manager does not automatically appeal to all people, despite the higher financial rewards. There is an increasing desire among them for their own career path to be separate from the management ladder. Not only are they concerned by the hassles of people management, but also by the rapid move away from applying skills they acquired through previous study and experience. Yet most employers show limited awareness of the need for alternative career paths and few are doing anything to change their management-oriented career path structures.

eg . promoting a specialist into a largely people —m/ment role

Uneasiness with your current occupation may be because you really want to operate at a higher level within it. Perhaps you need to take some action to help a promotion become a reality rather than subject yourself to the traumas of changing employers in the same field, or a total career change.

Although many people consider themselves ambitious, surprisingly few play an active role in preparing themselves for promotion. When they look at the jobs of their superiors, people often underestimate the requirements of additional knowledge and skill which such jobs demand. Many frequently stress the importance of the technical knowledge in a management job and overlook the study preparation and personal qualities needed for effective leadership, administration and financial control.

Since knowledge mostly derives from experience (your own or someone else's), the intelligent promotion hunter should seize every opportunity of being exposed to problems and situations which extend their knowledge and skill. You should encourage your superior to delegate challenging assignments, perhaps in the form of short-term projects. You may, for example, offer to carry out a special investigation of a long-standing problem which others have not had time to tackle. You may volunteer to take on a failing situation and turn it into a success.

There is to better way in which individuals can prepare themselves and earn promotion to the superior's job than by learning about its problems at first hand. To cope with the extra load, you will need to organize your work effectively.

Even if your manager is not good at delegating, you can ask questions about problems you observe; this will, at the very least, demonstrate your enthusiasm. Provided you are tactful in the way you go about obtaining insights you will, in most cases, find your manager increasingly willing to delegate and to share experiences. After all, it is very much in the manager's interest to find a competent successor; frequently it is the lack of a suitable replacement which causes managers to miss out on a promotion.

A planned reading program is a way of improving your chances, but there is a bewildering variety of books from which to choose. When it comes to the actual selection of suitable reading matter, there are plenty of sources of help. Your employer's training officer may be able to provide guidance and the information services staff of professional associations are usually willing to help. Another valuable source is the local library, staffed by people who are trained to select reading lists and to give research guidance.

> ### Self-development should be your concern. What you do for yourself is likely to make you more eligible for promotion.

Many people are members of professional associations, yet only a minority play any active part in their meetings and functions. If you are in search of self-improvement, participate enthusiastically in the work of the local branch, taking every opportunity to listen to experts in the field and discuss their presentations. At the same time, you will want to discuss common problems with others from different organizations. In this way, as on any effective training course, people contribute to their end and to each other's at the same time.

Your problem may not be lack of promotion or even lack of belief in the validity of your current occupation. You may just have been in it too long. The more experience you acquire, the easier it becomes to solve problems — particularly problems you have tackled and solved many times before. A promotion may result in a different set of problems and hence renewed challenge, or it could be profitable to think of a different career path within your current occupation.

Ambition and desire for promotion are encouraged — and even insisted upon — by employers. It is inferred that if we do not display these qualities and continue to progress up the ladder, we are no longer a worthwhile employee. This emphasis on progression through promotion is not shared by every employee. Many question the quality and real value of more senior responsibilities. The higher pay appears to many to be inadequate compensation for the apparent need to compromise value systems and sometimes even surrender personal integrity. Somehow, the propaganda about ambition and promotions has assumed that if we work hard to achieve our employer's goals a miracle of self-actualization — a high degree of personal fulfillment — will automatically occur.

In many cases, promotion to a higher level of job tasks can bring a renewed sense of satisfaction with your career. It may also result in a realization that you have overstepped your capabilities. It can be an important indicator of the wisdom of your career choice. In other words promotion can mean many things at different times in your working life.

Ambition

Seeking promotion will not always solve a job dissatisfaction problem. Striving for the top is something that many are beginning to question as a healthy objective. Promotion is often linked with long hours of work, high stress, domestic turbulence and, in many cases, poor health. The frequency of obituaries in our newspapers for executives who have died before reaching retirement age reinforces these concerns. A different attitude appears to be growing: one in which the individual believes he or she should have the freedom and responsibility not only to make a living, but also to make a life.

I have arrived

I have not seen the plays in town
   only the computer printouts
I have not read the latest books
   only The Wall Street Journal
I have not heard the birds sing this year
   only the ringing of phones
I have not taken a walk anywhere
   but from the parking lot to my office
I have not shared a feeling in years
   but my thoughts are known to all
I have not listened to my own needs
   but what I want I get
I have not shed a tear in ages
   I have arrived
Is *this* where I was going?

Natasha Josefowitz
Is This Where I Was Going?
(Columbus Books)

Many perceive ambition as causing a conflict between liking the people with whom they work and competing fiercely with them for advancement — sometimes by less than ethical means. Ambition implies a hard-driving individual who feels a constant pressure to get things done and is always racing against the clock. Ambitious people are often restless and have difficulty with idleness. They speak fast, move, walk and eat quickly and show impatience with the rate at which most events take place. They are often a coronary risk and are unlikely to spare adequate quality time for their partners and children. John Oliver Hobbes summed it up by saying: "A man with a career can have no time to waste upon his wife and friends, he feels he has to devote it wholly to his enemies."

These characteristics are causing many to question their desire for promotion and to reassess which activities in life they really value. Often this is accompanied by a new concern about employment security, as so few employers show sensitivity to or understanding for those who voluntarily remove themselves from the race up the pyramid structure. A change of employer, and sometimes occupation, is often necessary for those who wish to modify or redirect their ambitions.

Career plateau

Success and well-being are not the family norms; struggle and subservience are. Succeed only a little; too much success is dangerous, so the individual must withdraw . . . the norm becomes inaction, procrastination and confusion.

If your career has reached a plateau, pause to consider why. Is it because of factors outside your control, such as no visible opportunities for progress with your current employer? Is it because the skills for managing your own career require attention in order to compete successfully with your colleagues or external applicants? Or is it because you don't really want to move to more senior level jobs?

Careers can plateau for many reasons. Since there are fewer jobs than aspiring applicants for the more senior responsibilities within our pyramid-shaped employer organization, regular upward mobility is unlikely for many. There is not enough room at the top for all promotion hunters.

Self-honesty can be the hardest thing to achieve in the management of our careers. Many preach that to stop being ambitious — to plateau a career voluntarily — is a negative decision. But how many marriages, parent and child relationships, psychosomatic illnesses and psychological problems would be improved if there were more self-honesty and personal courage about this issue!

Being honest with yourself may lead to the decision to make a career change. Or you may decide to stay in your current occupation but to change employers. You may discover you need to learn how to manage your career plateau in order to survive within your current employment environment without the disapproval of others in power positions.

There is no reason why you cannot remain effective and capable of performing your job tasks while *not* seeking further promotion.

It does not mean ceasing personal growth nor your efforts to develop your job skills. It does mean skillfully informing your boss of this change in your attitude without conveying a lowering of enthusiasm or energy towards achieving the employer's objectives. But the first issue is the decision you make about yourself. The second is the strategy to inform others without incurring threat to your employment status.

"Plateauing," writes Judith Bardwick in her book, *The Plateauing Trap* (Allen & Unwin), "is a simple phenomenon, but it has been largely unrecognized so it's hard for people to talk about." She points out that plateauing is not necessarily bad, but it is emotionally depleting when the plateau results in the feeling that work or relationships or life have no momentum.

People who are plateaued have to create new opportunities by which they can restore self-esteem. What you have to do is change your aspirations, as well as some aspects of the work you do. You must also change some of the ways you live. You need to:

- be willing for change to happen. In other words, don't resist change, don't insist on clinging to the way things have always been;

- create new ambitions — admit that the old ones are no longer assets;

- accept the risks — this means you must be willing to take on some amount of uncertainty;

- let go of past habits — acknowledge that while gains were created, they also incur profound costs;

- be patient — remember that the transition phases in life ordinarily take two to three years because changing in basic ways is hard.

Financial appraisal

There are a few decisions about life which do not involve money; career management is not one of them. The money factor will influence your career decision, whether you are embarking on new college education studies, changing your lifestyle, sorting out financial planning for your retirement and possibly relocating your home.

When people appraise themselves there is a tendency to be too severe so that the overall self-assessment is negative. Often this occurs when appraising one's own financial assets, but for different reasons. What many see as a liability — for example, an annual insurance policy premium — a person trained in accounting will see as an asset for its borrowing power and/or surrender value. It's wise to seek relevant professional help for your financial appraisal. A person, such as your bank manager, can assess your true asset and liability position more quickly and accurately than you are likely to, unless you are trained in accounting. Another advantage of professional help can be advice on consolidating debts, extending loan terms, or predicting a net earnings level through reappraisal of income tax deductions and changes in gross income. It's an important aspect of career management strategy and demands accurate data to help sort out the facts in preparation for decision making and by whom and when they should be made.

The longer a person has been with one employer the greater likelihood there will be apprehension and reluctance about changing jobs and employer because of financial ties. These can take the form of equity in a pension fund, low interest home purchase loan or a partially or fully maintained car. In many cases, a person wanting a career transition abandons the quest for an alternative job on the basis that a change will cost too much. Most make that decision without sufficient research. For example, the trust deeds of many pension funds contain vesting and portability clauses which enable a member to transfer equity into a similar fund with a different employer. Many firms allow departing staff to take over leases on company cars; others have personnel policies which permit a person terminating employment to repay a loan with adjusted interest rates, so avoiding refinancing of the debt. It pays to research before you cancel a career transition objective solely on financial grounds and allow your frustration with your current worklife situation to continue.

A competent financial adviser should be involved to study your particular situation. Following such a discussion, you may well conclude that a cash lump sum payout of your pension contributions is in your best interest if you are going to reinvest the proceeds in suitable ways. Rather than being an obstacle, this can often facilitate a career transition.

Most will face the money issue as they consider desirable and potentially achievable career alternatives. The fact you must face up to is that you may need to lower your income level during the initial period of the transition. The compensation, while not material, is to be found in doing or working towards what you want to do rather than what you feel compelled to do.

How many workaholics have asked their partners what they would like to see them doing? Many would be surprised at the response. Supportive spouses are more likely to opt for the inner contentment of their companion in life than the continual striving for material gain and status. The latter frequently results in tension, ill health and deterioration in family life.

Those intending to change their current worklife patterns could benefit from some introspection about their parents and childhood. People usually respond to my questions on this in counselling situations with feelings about their childhood relationship with parents in qualitative terms, rarely material.

So, in the evolution of your life, will your children regard you in these terms? Not so much by the salary level you secured but more by the behavior you displayed during their formative years? The time shared with them? A parent with goals sorted out, who has life so arranged that time is provided for attention to the children and participation in their activities will more likely earn their respect and companionship as they grow up.

Money issues appear less critical when seen through the perceptions and needs of partners and children — those who are dear to us. To understand them you have to share with them your feelings, your frustrations, your hopes . . . and don't forget to ask their opinions!

Work and leisure

Career and life management planning involves analyzing what we really want to do and what is realistic in our leisure time, as well as in our work time. The notion that life's journey starts with Education, leads on to Work and then to Leisure (Retirement) is outdated. Leisure management is for now, whatever our age. It requires the same degree of effort, self-honesty, personal motivation and structured self-search to determine the content of our leisure as is necessary for our worklife. Both projects should be carried out concurrently. Both are likely to lead to making changes in what we do as we seek the best variety of alternative futures for ourselves. We alone decide the combination of work and leisure options.

Leisure has not occurred overnight as a specialist topic for life management focus. It has been with us for some time. A growing number of people are seeking ways to make their work and leisure interests contribute equally to the quality of their living.

There are adult and community education centers and associations across the country, that include many leisure topics within their programs in which adults are participating. They exist in response to the demand to stimulate, support and address the learning needs and interests of adults and to pursue the ideal of the development of the whole person.

Tapered Retirement

Pending retirement should involve career planning. Retirement activity choices are increasing — many producing income. The following illustrates them:

- Interrupted retirement: six months' vacation, followed by return to another position with the same or another employer.
- Phased retirement: lesser responsibilities with the same employer, phased down over a three- to five-year period.
- Ad hoc contract retirement: (for example, contract arrangement for same or other employer for two to five years).
- Semi-retirement: part-time job with the same or a similar employer (for example, a position as a consultant).
- Recall pool retirement: on contact list of former employer for recall for temporary job assignments, to stand in for others on leave or for specific short-term projects.
- Consulting retirement: a consulting, production or service business: part-time, full-time or job-sharing arrangement.
- "Dream" retirement: new career, part-time or full-time.
- Volunteer retirement: pursue volunteer work in the community.
- Avocation retirement: pursue an income-generating activity that has not been part of your employment history but may have been pursued outside working hours (for example, a hobby or interest).
- Leisure retirement: retire to extend your leisure activities.

Leisure is not simply nonwork, but activities with many aspects. It is not an abstract term. It contains the power for personal growth, the choice of companionship, coping better and relaxation. It has opportunities to explore vocational interests which may later be transferred to our worklife, or vice-versa, and expand our range of knowledge, skills and people whose company we enjoy. Leisure is a self-determined activity, or series of activities, available due to our having discretionary time. The activity may be physical, social, intellectual, creative or a combination of these. It has the capability of renewing our energy, refreshing our outlook on life's many travails and setbacks, allowing us to be more our real selves, with less of a requirement to role play that many employment settings influence us to do.

The search for our particular set of leisure activities should not be with the intent that they should compensate for tolerating unsatisfactory worklife. Work and leisure are both the source of life satisfactions. A career is, in effect, an interaction of work and leisure with varying degrees of importance at various times in our life's journey. One does not contrast the other; in fact, seen in this way, the similarities in work and leisure are emphasized, not the differences.

The joy of work

The attitudes that prevail in our society are incongruent with what I have learned about the joy of finding fulfilling work. The current view is that one should work neither too hard nor too much; that enjoyable times in living are reserved for weekends or vacations; that work is drudgery and thankless; that bosses are necessary for telling me how I am doing; that I am one person at work and a different person outside work. I find my work a joy. I believe others can do so with the right amount of personal effort. Persistence, stubbornness and gritty determination characterize this effort. I believe that our economy can benefit from people finding this joy and working enthusiastically and more productively.

Work for me is a creative experience, a deeply valuable pursuit. It has hardships, setbacks and irritations, but these are less of a bother to me. My energy levels are consistently high. I amaze myself by the amount of work I accomplish. I am working at what I really enjoy. Time with my family, trips to the countryside are scheduled into my day, not set aside to a specific period in each year. Work is an activity which allows me to use the more truthful parts of me — my real self.

The present concerns me more than the future. Work is a fulfilling expression of who I really am. The pressures, time demands and fluctuating financial circumstances are part of this joy. None is pleasurable in isolation, but as part of the whole scheme of things, each is an integral part of this experience.

Work provides me with a synergy of the skills I prefer using; there are many skills I have, and used well in the past, which I no longer use, nor want to. I am being selfish in what I do and in turn feel selfless in the way my work benefits others. I am well aware of my weaknesses, but do not dwell on them. I work with my strengths. I am never angry about my work, but rather it is the avenue through which I express my developing personality. I express my positive emotions through what I do. I am determined to do what I choose to do even though financial rewards beckon from other directions. Yes, I am addicted to my worklife. I do not crave status nor the approval of others. When it occurs, I enjoy the feeling, but I do not consciously seek it. I am not conceited about finding work I really like doing. I have paid a price to reach this state. I have earned the right to be joyful in what I do.

The danger of the past

A concoction of disillusionment, frustration, dissatisfaction, break-down in marriage, tumultuous living and desire to try a larger and more prospect-filled locality promoted me to migrate and alter the pattern of my career.

Whatever trauma each of us has experienced in our education, relationships or past employment, it is important to recognize that it is in the past and can distort our ability to focus on the future. Even today is tomorrow's past. Making a career move involves taking moderate risks. The possibility of disappointment or rejection by senior managers or by potential employers does exist and can never be fully eliminated.

It is likely that others will refer frequently to our past, particularly recruitment interviewers or selection panel members or managers at performance appraisal reviews.

The arousal of feelings of inadequacy about our education or inappropriate work experience must be guarded against. They must not be allowed to deter us from striving to achieve our objective. The fact that the past is past and cannot be changed must be incorporated into how we react. To be aware that the past has the power to poison our attitudes, behavior at work and responses to the criticisms of others can help us guard against it halting or hindering progress with our careers. The past is what we build on — not despair over.

Achieving
Career
Satisfaction

3-WHAT DO YOU REALLY WANT TO DO?

Redefining ourselves

Each of us has an individual world created around our view of self. This inward view of ourselves gives each of us our personal perspective on the world around us. The events occurring in the outside world, whether work, family or other happenings, are interpreted by the current state of our inner world or view of self. Some call this inner world our self-concept. Just as events are occurring outside us — a continual series of changes — our inner world is changing also. Therefore, our view of these external events changes as our sense of self changes and we modify our inward view as these changes take place.

The true nature of our career and its meaning for our inner world may not be the same for those who observe us, whether they are our loved ones, boss, counsellors, employment consultants or relatives. If we are promoted at work, others are likely to view it as an indicator of success. But inwardly we may view it as costing dearly in terms of our desire to have more time for personal projects of a nonwork nature. Being retrenched may appear to others as a setback while our inner self may feel relief that we no longer work in a particular set of work situations.

Our career, even further, our life, is the outcome of our inner self's responses to the interaction between these external and internal forces. The choices, decisions and emotional investments we make in work, family and other areas shape the overall nature of our living. Because neither we nor the environment stays still, changes in both influence, alter and sometimes disturb our viewpoint. Both major and trivial changes can disrupt the balance. A new accommodation needs to be made. A redefinition of self and our external world is required in order to restore comfort to our living and a sureness that the actions we take are really right for us. New assessments, and expanded awareness of strengths, skills, preferences and value systems need to be made. Hence our career is a sequence of alternating stable and transitional phases.

To deal effectively with these transitional phases we need to pause and take stock. Many of us do not bother to do this. As individuals we are often uncomfortable in changed, unbalanced situations and seek quickly to reduce the discomfort of our thoughts. We often accept the first job offer if we are out of work. With the loss of inner identity in a job or career path with a particular employer and the future we anticipated within it abruptly gone, we are prone to urgency in attempts to replace what we have lost. The sense of self, fractured by our external world, needs healing before rational decision making can take place. But rarely do we give this a chance. We tend to want to bring the present uncomfortable phase to a close a soon as possible by accepting any option available to us.

How may this balance between our inner world and the interacting forces with these external events be restored? Most of us look outside ourselves for the answer. We apply rapidly for jobs. We enroll in new courses after losing out on a promotion in order to increase our chances the next time round. We go on holidays with our severance pay in the hope that the answer to what we should do will occur while we are away from our normal surroundings and in pleasant conditions. We sell things —sometimes treasured personal items — so that we feel better because some money is coming in. The action is more important to us than the amount of money we receive.

Our perspective on what has occurred in our external world influences the way we set about mending our shattered inner state. Often, our dominant concern is to react as we think the observers of our behavior think we should. At this critical point we tend to worry more about them than about redefining ourselves.

Most of this redefinition has to be done alone, although other people can be important reference points to help sort out your thoughts. Yet the internal "homework" needs to be done — at least advanced quite some way — before you should elicit their help. It can be a lonely period. A period of turbulence and a mental tug-of-war between inclinations, logic, rationality, escapism, emotions, responsibilities and our perspectives of the expectations of others close to us. A veritable maze of conflicts and a jigsaw of confusions. Our emotional equilibrium is gone and our self-confidence and feelings of self-regard appear to be on a roller coaster ride. One moment level and calm, the next in a whirlwind of contradictions and apprehension.

Action is needed here to sort the whole thing out. Action we take alone (self-assessment) and action we take with others (information gathering).

Self-assessment

Work satisfaction depends on several issues. One critical issue is to have a clear idea of the direction you really want to take. Attaining this clarity may be possible without help from others. You should try on your own first. If you do not succeed, it's common sense, not defeat, to seek professional help.

Career decisions cannot be made sensibly in isolation from your family. If no dependent family is involved then your total lifestyle needs reappraisal before you commit yourself to a new occupational direction. Whether married, single, or in a relationship, you should think about work and leisure and how they affect your values and obligations to others. How much of your life at present is dominated by your occupation? Is what you feel you have to do, what you want to do? How far does work intrude into your private life? Have you analyzed the true amount of the discretionary time you have to do what you please, after deducting time required for work, commuting, domestic chores and physiological needs?

You may need to keep a detailed diary of each day's events over a month to appraise accurately how your time is being spent. The issues then become clearer. Do you want more discretionary time or are you prepared to sacrifice some for part-time study or a longer time allocated to work? Deciding what kind of change you need is essential before researching possible alternative occupational directions. It's essential because you may just find that your occupation does not really need to change but other aspects of your life require altering. This self-appraisal has a great bearing upon the kind of work you might enjoy and succeed at if a career path change is the conclusion you reach.

So deciding if and what kind of change is required, determining your aptitudes and interests, matching them with types of occupations, validating whether they are available in the current employment scene, then obtaining your new job, is the exciting journey on which you are embarking.

It is important that you follow a structured program to help you analyze honestly your skills and needs in a career. Some people prefer and have access to training courses led by experienced counsellors. Courses are a highly supportive and low-risk environment in which to conduct such self-exploration. Many of the "graduates" of the courses I conduct willingly pledge to support one another in implementing their new plans.

For those who do not have access to such training or who prefer not to follow such a method, responding to carefully structured guidelines is an effective way of finding out what you can and would like to do.

I have provided such guidelines in Part Two. You can follow them in your own home, at your own pace and when you feel that your motivation is at its optimum level. You need peace and quiet so that you can concentrate — and you need to be honest and realistic. Pace yourself sensibly, so that the process of discovering what is right and what is wrong, what should be changed and what can be changed, does not result in anger and despair, but in a feeling that you are in control of your life —and can change it.

Completion of ten or more of the career analysis exercises which follow should first be a solo activity. But discussion with others can make the process more productive. They can often identify aspects of your experience and skills of which you may not be fully aware. You may also need to be reassured that some of your conclusions are correct.

You will need to spend a considerable amount of time.

Your search has many dimensions. Learning is change, problem solving, reorganizing experiences; it often involves "unlearning" and is hard work, but will result in personal growth. Just as you have matured by learning from the experiences of living, so this analysis activity is simply an extension of that process. Much may take place that impedes the development of your career goal. Treat these irritations in the same way as you do commuting hassles, full in-trays, missed buses or trains — by realizing that they are a necessary part of living and contribute to your appreciation and enjoyment of life's more pleasurable experiences and events.

A career, like a business, requires management. Those who complete career analysis discover the substantial amount of control which is within their reach. Tasks such as setting objectives, identifying strengths and weaknesses, developing and maintaining skills, and formulating and implementing worklife strategies — all these career management skills must be brought into play.

Many have learned to tackle their career transition by following the structured approach in Part Two of this book; it provides a consistent focus for self-questioning and disciplines the progress of thought. Such an approach requires a thorough analysis of your capabilities and preferences in order to plan for a more fulfilling worklife. The answer to a more satisfying future is in your hands.

The task is to examine yourself in the most thorough way possible; to identify all your skills; select those you enjoy using the most; and identify an employment occupation, career path and work environment in which there is the greatest likelihood of self-fulfillment. Then you need to set out confidently to persuade others to promote or employ you.

The increased sense of well-being that emanates from people who have taken time to sort out their career directions is a wonderful thing to observe. The extracts from correspondence in my files give some clue to the therapeutic value of solving career dilemmas. These people were not defeated by the apparent difficulty — they faced up to it and broke through it!

A forty-five-year-old: "I knew something was wrong in my career. I had been reasonably successful but there always seemed to be a strain. I realized after analyzing who I really was that I needed to change from a commercial and profit-minded organization to one more concerned with providing a professional service. Then I could feel that my work was worthwhile."

A thirty-six-year-old: "I had enjoyed a very successful technical career, but had to consider what happened once I left the laboratory. Career analysis helped me sort out the choices and recognize that I had the personality and outlook which would suit a career in technical marketing."

A thirty-nine-year-old: "I was laid off at thirty-eight, having been in the same job for fifteen years. It was a great shock, and I was very resentful. Once I had talked through the situation I realized that it gave me an opportunity to establish myself in a completely different career much more suited to my interest and abilities."

A married woman aged forty-two: "Not having studied or worked for twenty years I had no confidence in myself. Aptitude tests showed that I could study degree level subjects, and career counselling revealed that I had the right abilities and personality to qualify and train as a social worker. My successful first semester results are the best news I've had for many years."

A serviceman aged thirty-six: "I am due to leave the military at thirty-eight, and am very glad I undertook career analysis. Now I can begin a correspondence course with confidence to prepare me for a career as a purchasing officer. The analysis of my aptitudes and interests showed that I would be very suited to such a career."

A fifty-three-year-old: "I had been very successful at the cost of working long hours. I now recognize that I have no real will to continue in the rat race and get to the top. Instead, I can now lower my sights with comfort, leaving me with much more time to be with my family and to develop the hobbies and interests that I could never satisfy in my job."

A forty-eight-year-old: "It gave me the confidence and encouragement to take the plunge and become self-employed. I will be giving up a secure job with a good pension, but use of your career analysis methods showed that I had a good chance of gaining real success and satisfaction in my career by starting up my own business."

Male — twenty-nine years of age: "I would finally like to say to anyone who has the same feelings that I had, not to be afraid to go out there and achieve what you want. The key factor is self-analysis and confidence and not to let past failures get you down. If you have enough determination you will reap the rewards and find exactly what you are looking for."

> ▓ *If you, too, respond to the challenge* ▓
> *and work hard and conscientiously*
> *through the rest of this book, you will find*
> *work satisfaction within your reach.*

Three-dimensional approach

> *I have discovered that a good job is secondary to a good life. Enjoyment comes from yourself and from your attitudes to job and life, not just from what you do for a living.*

The process of identifying the right direction for our career transition has more complexity than simply identifying aptitudes, that is, the skills to perform a particular job at a particular level of intelligence.

Career analysis necessitates a three-dimensional approach with focus on each of the following in turn: Job Content, Employment Environment and Lifestyle Preference. Once data has been assembled for each of these, the task of integrating the indicators from each into a coherent career direction is addressed. When this has been carried out and relevant decisions made, the examination, choice and implementation of a specific career strategy takes place.

A person's career is an integration of lifestyle, employment environment and job content needs. Job content can be described as a specific set of tasks containing some which are preferred and others tolerated or demoralizing. The employment environment is as important as job content in defining what is wanted because it affects the psychological aspects of work such as degree of independence, self-concept, security and interpersonal relationships with work colleagues and management. A career, however, will affect most, even all, of a person's life. The job content and employment environment largely determine the standard of living, including where we live, our recreational activities, schools our children attend, and clothing and transportation choices. The actions a person takes to enhance these three dimensions of their living is career development and life management. Each person has characteristics which cause them to be satisfied or dissatisfied in relation to each of these three dimensions of job content, employment environment and lifestyle needs.

Our data gathering must relate to each of the three dimensions and be integrated with the career self-help action we must then take if worklife improvement is genuinely desired. Although information gathering about alternatives is essential, the time and resources to explore all options is rarely possible: therefore, at some point a decision is made and action taken relating to it.

Transferable skills

Compiling an inventory of all your skills and capabilities is a necessary, exciting and difficult process. It is an essential part of improving the management of your career. How to do this is described in Part Two.

You need to identify all your skills and recognize their potential for transfer to different career situations. Without a full appraisal of what

Sample of a Person's
Three-Dimensional Analysis Summary

Job Content

- Varied, non-routine
- Creative
- Some analysis/problem solving
- Worthwhile results — social value
- Some flexibility (not straight 9 a.m. to 5 p.m.)
- Assisting others
- Some teaching/training component
- Some individual (one-to-one) in-depth dealings
- Adventure/excitement
- Opportunity for personal growth (self and knowledge)
- Challenge
- Dealing with a broad range of people
- Opportunity for individual expression

Employment Environment

- Nonbureaucratic
- Open/common goals
- Variable location of job tasks (not stuck in the office)
- Small rather than large organization
- Private rather than public service
- Dealing with people (group and individual)
- Offers some independence (creating opportunities)
- Not have to conform to the "executive image" (at least not all the time)
- Developing ideas with others — sharing approaches
- Being able to make a deal (something I can believe in)

Lifestyle Preference

- Work/leisure balance (time for the family)
- Probably smaller city environment (more relaxed)
- Not suburbia
- A sense of community
- Variable work time
- Being able to share some common goals
- Being in charge of my own destiny
- Reduced stress and anxiety levels
- Perhaps involving significant other or sharing some venture
- Definitely not conforming to the upwardly mobile successful urban family unit

you are capable of, it is not practical to try to select goals that can be achieved and are relevant to your worklife well-being.

As you consider each identified skill, a check must be made that your self-perception is correct. Proof of these skills needs to be found in evidence from your current and past activities. If you have used the skill successfully, you can verify that it does indeed represent a capability.

The search for all your skills has additional benefits in the selection of alternative career strategies. As your inventory of skills expands, you become more able to describe who you really are in worklife terms, what you merit and why. As many career management actions require that other people be convinced of your merits, this enhanced ability to communicate the basis of your claims for consideration is an important bonus.

A further benefit is the growth in self-confidence as the search process reveals that your skills are much more extensive than you previously thought.

In my experience in career guidance for adults, everyone has found convincing evidence of the validity of their skills inventory, improved self-esteem and a greater range of career options, providing the hard work of self-assessment has been earnestly undertaken.

Our perception of ourselves is an important determinant of our worklife behavior. There is a risk in managing our career effectively if we have inadequate knowledge about ourselves. Yet everything known and not known about ourselves can be grouped into four categories. Two psychologists, Joe Luft and Harry Ingham, designed a model called the Johari Window to demonstrate this.

The Johari Window can be used to increase self-understanding in the following way. The first quadrant OPEN indicates that there is a part of you that is known to both you and the people with whom you are regularly involved. It represents information about yourself which you know and others also know. The second quadrant BLIND suggests that there is a part of you which others are aware of but which is currently unknown to you. You do need to find out about this area in order to implement effective career strategies. Your endeavors on your own with the aid of the skills search and the data gathering exercises will help here, yet the real value is in sharing and checking with others about your discoveries. Their feedback may help you amend or confirm your findings.

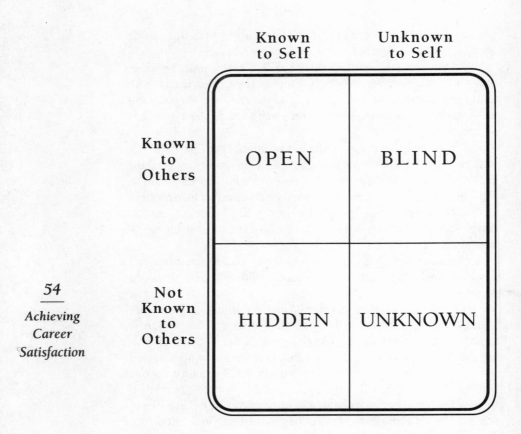

The Johari Window

The third quadrant HIDDEN is just the reverse of the second one. Here you know something about yourself — your attitudes, values, motives, feelings or capabilities — that you don't readily reveal to others. However, you need to be prepared to share some facts about this part of yourself or you will limit the opportunity to find out whether your self-concept is complete and accurate.

Finally, the fourth quadrant UNKNOWN indicates that there are parts of you that are unknown to both you and others, unless a determined effort is made to examine what is there. You need to clear away a part of this opaque or "walled up" area.

In the quadrants of the Johari Window most of the data necessary for prudent career action steps can be found. Determination to conduct such a search must be a prerequisite to the journey of self-discovery and increased self-awareness.

Most people manage to find the time, motivation and personal industry needed to assemble this inventory when they are intent on improving their worklife. But the factor which frequently threatens the success of the self-assessment process is modesty. Years of conditioning by others when modesty about our talents was highlighted as a virtue can be a stubborn obstacle to success. To present ourselves to others as modest inhibits our ability to acknowledge our accomplishments. And, as each of our accomplishments required a particular set of skills, to refrain from acknowledging all of them proudly and in detail will hide many precious skills and capabilities from our personal search.

What is a skill?

In Part Two, there are a wide range of exercises to guide your self-exploration. Most of the exercises are designed so that you can complete them in the privacy of your home. Whether searching for skills alone or in partnership with friends, acquaintances, managers, career counsellors or loved ones, you need to make the following resolutions before you begin:

- I will judge the existence of a skill by my own standards and satisfaction.

- I will detect several individual skills in everything I do and have done.

- I acknowledge that once a skill has been used, however long ago, I will always have it to call upon.

- I commit myself to the need to complete the inventory of all my skills, then to work hard at rearranging my skills in:

  (i) terms of those I enjoy using, even though in some cases I may not use them very well;

  (ii) a variety of configurations which will provide insight into alternative sets of job tasks appropriate to my uniqueness as a human being.

At this stage, you may be eager to launch into the self-exploration process without further delay. But stay with me for just a few moments more. Let's study this term "skill", as it obviously has great importance to the quest for worklife satisfaction. For the purpose of career analysis, I have found that one definition alone is not adequate. In my opinion, the following statements provide the best composite explanation of a skill:

- a specific behavior that results in an achievement;

- ways in which you tend to be successful when dealing with problems, tasks and other life experiences;

- characteristics that give you the ability to do something;

- attributes used in dealing with DATA (analyzing, compiling), PEOPLE (persuading, negotiating, supervising) and THINGS (handling, driving, operating);

- qualities, traits, talents which are used in living each day;

- activities which you may do with great difficulty, some difficulty or easily; (You do not have to do things easily in order to have a skill.)

- a capacity, a natural gift, an instinct, an eye for, an ear for, a knack, a proficiency, a handiness or a strong point.

You should return to these skill definitions frequently when completing the career analysis exercises which follow in Chapters 5 and 6 in order to trigger new areas of search.

Some of our skills become evident early in life, such as mathematical ability, musical talent or agility in sports. Most skills develop slowly and are more difficult to recognize. Many relate to ways of interacting with people, such as public speaking, organizing or supervising. Several skills, such as being methodical, talkative or inquisitive, can often be less desirable in the eyes of others. Yet using these so-called less desirable skills in certain types of jobs can result in both effective and satisfying work performance. They should not be ignored or passed over hurriedly as you seek to extend your personal skills inventory. Grouped with some of your other skills, the combined effect could be an important indicator of new areas of potential work satisfaction.

Needs, wants, values, personal strengths and limitations —these are the factors on which worklife satisfaction is built. Unless we pause to take stock of each of these in turn, then integrate them into an overall plan and series of resolutions, any quest for such satisfaction will be futile.

The self-analysis exercises in Part Two have two objectives. The first is to help you become aware of each relevant aspect of yourself so that you can make informed choices about your worklife. The second is to build your self-esteem. By discovering your strengths, appreciating your achievements and clarifying what is realistic, your self-esteem and your self-confidence rise.

At the conclusion of the exercises, you should write a statement about your understanding of the results of the data revealed through your self-analysis and work. Your writings should comment on how the results could be used in your personal growth and career planning.

Planning your career

Career analysis is the initial process of finding out enough about yourself to make informed decisions about your choice of occupation and the types of working environment and lifestyle factors in which you have improved opportunities for satisfaction.

Setting a course for a fulfilling future, however, requires more than this. The aim at this stage is to consolidate what you are learning about your real needs to examine how this information may be used to achieve specific career action steps and a greater sense of inner well-being. Career planning is identifying what strategies are necessary to succeed.

Developing a career plan has several potential benefits:

- All manner of unexpected events may arise about which a worklife-related decision must be made — often quickly. A recorded plan will help you decide what is in your best interest at the time the decision needs to be made.

- It helps you to decide whether your expectations and schedule are realistic.

- A plan will go a long way towards providing you with emotional peace of mind. A plan makes you feel more secure and less prone to worry about what has not yet occurred.

- It enables you to asses different ways to achieve your goals.

- When written down against time schedules, a plan becomes a means of measuring how well you are doing at regular intervals based on your own assessment, not the opinions of others.

Career planning is a personal process of planning one's future worklife. You start with what you would like to do and refine a plan consisting of what you are capable of doing. It involves deciding on what developmental action should be taken and determining how to incorporate your objectives with the expectations and requirements of an employer.

As we continuously change in what is important to us through different stages of our lives, career planning has to be a continuous process. It needs to be examined regularly and reassessed in the light of changing needs, employment situations and our expectations from work.

What career planning is NOT is relying solely on employers to look after this aspect of our lives. That's not their purpose nor proper role. Organizations exist to serve the objectives which evolved from the reasons for their creation. It is unrealistic to expect employers to divert energy and attention from the achievement of these objectives by attending to every need we have in relation to our worklife.

Career development support

An employer which does not provide some facilities to help us progress with our plans is being neglectful. Consequences of neglect are usually high labor turnover, absenteeism, unsatisfactory productivity, poor quality products or service to customers and low morale.

Useful career planning help from your employer should include:

- performance appraisal feedback by competent supervisors;

- provision of counselling facilities;

- conduct of training courses to assist exploration of your career needs;

- evidence of supportive encouragement from people in management positions;

- educational assistance and skills development training programs.

Managers need information in order to make effective managerial decisions about matters which affect our careers. This information should come from their managers and support staff but, equally importantly, from you. When career planning support is not available, you need to evaluate your position. If, after careful thought — not emotionally driven haste — you decide to resign, then both you and the employer are better off.

Many employers are cautious about providing career support facilities and procedures. Their concern is often that the career expectations of their employees may be raised to a point where it is not practical to help fulfill them. Nevertheless, career planning support should take place so that the employee/employer relationship is a compatible one, not antagonistic or resentful. Whatever the nature of your employer's support, your responsibility which cannot be abdicated is to:

- find out the employer's real expectations of you;

- set career objectives which are integrated with the employer's requirements;

- consider the opportunities available within their employ;

- make decisions about the career path direction you would like to follow.

You must be self-reliant in planning your life and then seek a cooperative relationship with your employer. Unless information on career paths and possible rewards are provided by your employer, you may fill the gap with assumptions which may be erroneous — and you could make decisions which do not work out or even leave their employ unnecessarily.

The challenge for the employer is to learn how to assist you to learn about yourself and the realities of organizational life. It is not doing the total career planning task for you. Your manager should help by providing you with information on opportunities and developmental resources.

If, after a very thorough analysis and checking, you conclude your employer can't help you, then you can turn to an alternative employment environment with the comfort that your decision has been made in a well-reasoned, logical and efficient manner.

■ By completing the career planning ■
exercises in Part Two you will establish
for your occupational activities:

- *priorities, plans and realistic reward expectations about your worklife;*

- *specific career path targets and what developmental activities you need to help you meet them;*

- *a schedule for achieving what you want.*

Forming your goals

To allow your desire for an improved worklife to remain just a desire is to deny the full value of the work you have undertaken in the career analysis and life management examination section. You have substantially enlarged your self-knowledge and proved to yourself your willingness and discipline to identify the problems and the solutions. The vital next step has to be charting what should happen in relation to your future worklife. To dream, fantasize, to await the fickleness of luck — these are not part of the strategy. It's back to the hard work of writing down specifics. Actionable objectives must be articulated and recorded in writing. Time schedules need to be assigned. There should be short-term objectives and long-term objectives. All must be attainable and the obstacles to their achievement clearly defined. Resources need to be identified — people, money, further education, etc.

Through each of the career planning exercises common threads will become evident. They are:

- your personal resources;

- your personal obstacles;

- your employment environmental obstacles;

- resources of your employer and other organizations or community services available to help you.

After you have completed the career planning exercises, you should write a summary of your situation under each of the above headings. This will help you label many factors that may affect accomplishing your new plans. For every career planning objective there are circumstances that hinder or help its achievement. Completing this summary will enable a special focus to be applied to each of them — whether or not they are factors which will contribute to or restrain achievement of the goal. Once these factors have been defined and analyzed you are likely to find that the obstacles appear less forbidding and the resources available to you more extensive than you may have first thought.

Information gathering

After considerable introspection and hard work you will have completed the preliminary self-search exercises and arrived at the point where you know the alternatives which are more suited to the skills you enjoy using in the type of work environment which will enhance your sense of well-being.

A common pitfall at this stage is to regard the targeting process as complete. Many initiate a vigorous job-searching campaign in order to bring about the transition to a more promising field of endeavor without further delay. The growth of self-awareness and self-confidence is deceptive. You may not have sufficient information to reduce the likelihood of an inappropriate change, nor accumulated all the necessary evidence to persuade employers to hire you into an occupation which may superficially contrast negatively with your past employment record. Before a career transition campaign is started, a period of reality testing and preparation of a career plan should be carried out as they are important components of the process.

The reality-testing process is a means of using information sources in order to verify whether an alternative is the most appropriate for you. The evidence you gather from your exploration and research can be used selectively to devise your career plan and later bolster the contents of your job application if one is required for your career transition. The more convincing your evidence of capabilities and belief in them, the more practical will be your plan to achieve new goals.

What inhibits people from carrying through the reality-testing phase of career analysis? First of all, you could be thinking that the true nature of an occupation cannot be identified without actually performing the tasks. Or that the true nature of an industry needs to be experienced to be understood. Neither are, in fact, obstacles to reality testing. Consider the wealth of information you can obtain from the following:

- People: You can make contact with people already in your targeted occupation, customers of and suppliers to the relevant industry; you can tap the information sources of the professional association for the occupation and the industry association which represents the employers in which it is located.

- Publications: Most industries publish information about their activities. Many employers feel compelled to rush into print and regularly update information about their activities and jobs for such reasons as public relations, shareholder information, export trade solicitations, government lobbying and consumer/supplier communication purposes. Annual reports, newsletters, house journals and codes of ethics are further examples of data you can readily obtain. It would be a strange organization which did not respond to a polite request from you. There is very little which is kept secret about the nature of occupations or the trading activities and objectives of employers.

- Imagine that you are an inquiring journalist or, if you prefer, a private detective. Put yourself in their shoes: how would such a person set about the task of obtaining information on career path options? The process of reality testing will become less inhibiting in this context. After all, you may be about to take the biggest risk of your life by changing from an occupation you know well — but dislike — to another with all the financial, emotional and status risks that the transition implies.

Supply and demand

It would be an unwise career planner who did not research the current and future availability of occupations. The task is not an easy one. The sources of information are varied and often contradictory about predictions on occupational demand. The more sources you seek in the quest for information, the more is available for analysis and forming conclusions. You need to search a variety of reference sources.

Demand in all occupations is influenced by a variety of factors. In some cases, sudden changes in government policies affecting expenditure can change the pattern of demand from year to year; for example, social workers are directly affected by the levels of government expenditure in health and welfare. Such areas as engineering will be affected more by the level of business confidence and construction or manufacturing activity. Others, like teaching, health care and dentistry, are affected by demographic factors.

There are several factors that will change the future job market. One is population growth. It will fuel demand for additional goods and services and new businesses and jobs will be created to meet the demand. Other factors are technological advances, new business practices and shifts in the needs and tastes of the public. You can monitor economic conditions in various regions of the country through the business pages of major newspapers and in the national business magazines.

You will need to look carefully at employers, as well as occupations. If an employer is financially sound and well managed and has a record of growth over the years, it can be expected to capture more business in the years ahead. The result will be new jobs and expanding career opportunities.

Another consideration when evaluating career prospects with a particular employer is the relationship of your career field to the organization's principal operations. The jobs vital to the functioning of the business will be most resistant to fallout from the bad periods that can affect any company from time to time. People in career fields which may be considered peripheral to profits, such as public relations, personnel and training, are often among the first to go when an employer contracts and retrenches in response to a financial crisis.

An important career advancement strategy is to research and evaluate the most likely employment environment in which you will be judged on your work performance and be noticed by others. For example, the visibility of individual performance to senior management is considerably improved in a small firm compared with the cavernous corridors and numerous offices of large organizations.

A considerable amount of career information is published for use by undergraduate college students. The mature-age career planner should not ignore this material. The more thorough the research, the more accurate will be your career plan.

Decision making

Where many people experience difficulties in career management is the decision making between two or more career direction options. It will help to spend some time now analyzing your decision-making habits. You can do this by looking at how you have made important decisions in the past.

First of all, you must believe that you do have quite a degree of control over your life and its direction. Of course, we all recognize that much of what happens to us in life occurs by chance — the family into which we were born, the town we grew up in, the educational opportunities we were given and many other events. However in everyone's life there are opportunities to do something with these experiences.

We have already made many decisions based on these experiences. It is important at this stage to look back at those decisions. If the manner in which you decided is not what it should have been, now is your opportunity to change it.

You may discover that many of your decisions were based on incorrect or insufficient information; you may not have made the effort to discover all the facts and options first. Timing may have been off; you may have made decisions too quickly, or too slowly. You may find that you were afraid to take risks that would have led you in desired directions. On the other hand, you may have taken too many risks or risks that were too great, with awkward results.

Looking back at your choice of education, partner, jobs, home, you may also be surprised to find that many things happened to you through inaction or by default. Your failure to make a decision was, in its own way, a decision.

Use the data you prepare in your career analysis which follows to help you list some of the important decisions you have made. Don't just focus on the outcome, but think about the process you used to arrive at those decisions. Ask yourself the following questions:

- Did you take enough time to define the issues clearly and completely?

- Did you look at all possible alternatives?

- Did you use the advice and help of friends, family and professionals as fully as you could, still making the final decision completely your own? If you didn't ask the right questions, you probably didn't get the right answers.

- Did you take reasonable risks; was your behavior timid or adventurous?

- What about your timing? Did you miss out on opportunities because of procrastination or rush into a decision without taking enough time to predict the likely consequences?

If you conclude that the way you have made past decisions was inadequate, now is the time to decide to make them more skillfully by completing the exercises in Chapter 8 with every ounce of energy and care you can apply.

Getting under way

Start by looking over what is required in each of the analysis and planning exercises in Part Two; each has practical activities from which you can learn and see things more clearly. Begin the task without procrastination. If one analysis method proves too difficult, select another. Search for those which provide the greatest comfort and ease in carrying out the self-analysis. There is no reason to hold back from expressing your thoughts in writing. No other person needs to read them unless you wish it.

With the extensive data you assemble you will find completing the different ways of developing career plans a rewarding exercise. The value of your hard work will be visible in the relative ease with which you can apply what you know about yourself to your future worklife.

The analysis exercises give you a unique chance to examine your abilities, skills and what you really value. The increase in self-knowledge you will acquire will enable you to make important decisions confidently about the career direction you should take. In this way you will radically reduce the chances of making inappropriate decisions. Knowing who you are and what you really want and merit must be tackled with honesty and vigor. Making this effort need not create awkward feelings — rather a pleasure of self-discovery.

What is required from you in the following exercises is based on a very sound fact — if you want to improve your situation you, and only you, can act on this desire.

Journey's end

I have described how you can conduct an objective, rational and systematic assessment of yourself and your career. This increase in self-knowledge can then be used to guide your search for information about job content, occupation and organizational possibilities. This information can be used to develop a number of personal themes and lead to writing statements that incorporate the key factors to be considered in deciding your next career actions. Through this search career action alternatives can be selected which fit your personal themes, goals and schedule.

The career transition journey is therefore a process of discovery. Because we change and so do our employment environments, this journey is not completed until we cease working. Yet we can take up the methods of personal review at any stage to ask ourselves: What do I want? What do they want? (The significant other, family, employer, boss.) What can, should and will I do? How will I get there?

New insights will be acquired each time we pause on the journey to undertake this review. When we initiate this review, rather than wait until a career setback thrusts the review upon us, we learn how to carry out life management — how to feel more in control of the nature of our journey.

I am immensely proud of my career transition graduates who followed the procedures I have described. People who elected not to be a victim of pinball living but set out to enact change in their lives. They:

- identified what was really important to their worklife;

- discovered their real strength/resources;

- used ingenuity to find opportunities;

- committed wholeheartedly to their career action steps;

- attuned their aspirations to reality;

- believed in their ability to improve their feelings about work.

I usually avoid providing an occupational title when a stranger asks me what I do. I prefer saying, "I help people arrive at a state where they say 'I like myself'." I have learned that when a person arrives at this point of self-comfort through my career transition guidelines, and the structured self-assessment and personal goal-setting procedures which follow in Part Two, all meaningful career transition actions take off.

67
___

What Do
You Really
Want to Do?

Career Analysis and Life Management Planning

Self-review is a reaching backward and forward in time through focused desire. Through written recollections you can gain self-knowledge, release delayed or repressed emotions, find hidden misconceptions that influenced your self-image, forgive and forget past offenses, and imaginatively explore roads taken and not taken to discover present fulfillment as well as future options.

Tristine Rainer
The New Diary

The only kind of learning which significantly influences behavior is self-discovered or self-appropriated learning — truth that has been assimilated in experience.

Carl Rogers

4- YOUR PREPARATION

Skills you will use

- Self-appraisal: Understanding who you really are and establishing what you really want from your worklife activities.

- Gathering Occupational and Employer Information: Getting the correct fit between you, your personal circumstances and your work.

- Problem Analysis: Choosing from alternatives developed from your self-appraisal and occupational research.

- Objective Setting/Scheduling: Selecting goals and the necessary career action steps consistent with your capabilities and clearly stated needs.

- Motivation to Implement Plans: Learning how to get started and maintain the momentum. Overcoming setbacks if they occur.

- Achievement Techniques: Identifying opportunities, gaining attention for your needs and convincing others of your worth.

Other essentials

- Desire to feel more "in charge" of your life.

- Time and privacy.

- Frank consultation with your partner and other people who will be affected by your decisions and the worklife changes you will make.

- A mentor with whom to test out your analyses, goals formed and proposed career action step plans.

- Detailed appraisal of your financial situation.

- Stress management techniques for emotional and physical health.

Your daily learning journal

During each day of your career analysis and life management planning journey it can be valuable to record in a journal key thoughts, ideas, issues and questions as they arise. These can be used later as refresher thoughts or links to ideas that occurred to you which may connect usefully with aspects and problems in your worklife. Your journal is a way of helping you to:

- capture ideas and visions for your career as they occur;

- write freely about yourself or, if you are so inclined, draw sketches, cartoons or diagrams when you want;

- analyze your frustrations, even anger and resentment;

- increase your perception and interpretation of what really is important to you.

In addition, recording in your journal develops your ability to express your ideas about people, incidents, things, dreams and significant events in your life. Use the following headings for entries in your journal each day:

- Learnings — write brief notes of the most significant concepts, principles or ideas learned during each day of your self-search period. This can be done during the day, but most people find that the late evening offers a better recording time for reviewing activities and thoughts, ideas, concepts and realizations.

- Applications or Actions — write brief notes on how your learnings might be applied or implemented by you; record things to start doing or stop doing.

- Things to Find Out More About — Record them. Questions may occur to you at inappropriate times when you are unable to find out the answer right away. They may be related to a desire to gain further clarification of a concept or procedure or may be queries you need to put to others about your worklife situation.

Your journal is a PRIVATE RECORD in which you can record honest notes about your feelings and attitudes and draft plans for the future. Reward yourself with an indulgence every now and then as you experiment with this uninhibited form of self-expression.

To start your daily learning journal:

- obtain a hard-backed notebook about 8" x 6" in size;

- always carry a few pieces of paper in your pocket, briefcase or handbag so that you can jot down ideas and thoughts at any time as they occur;

- build a pocket into the back of your journal to store these notes;

- each day spread out your papers and record this data in your journal;

- before you write in your journal, sit for five minutes with your eyes closed and concentrate on recalling the ideas and/or situations you wish to write about;

- write freely. Don't worry about the style of your writing. It's not essay writing for critical review by an expert in the English language, syntax and grammar!

▓ *You are about to focus on:* ▓

current questions and concerns; past events and themes; people in your life; real options and their implications; ways to take action.

Self-search through structured analysis

The career transition and life management journey you are about to commence is an exciting one. You will feel this as you participate in the process and follow the instructions each step of the way. Here is a chart to show you an overview of your journey.

Self-Assessment

⬇

Interpreting Data

⬇

Opportunity Awareness

⬇

Decision Learning

⬇

Transition Training

⬇

Successful Transition Accomplished

Steven's Model for Career Development

The Career Analysis and Life Management Planning Journey

Self-assessment

Clarifying Issues and Concerns→ Assembling Information Base through Structured Analysis → Education and Employment Experiences→ Abilities → Interests→ Values→ Primary Wants→ Employment Environment Preferences→ Lifestyle Considerations→ Biographical Review

Interpreting Data

Analysis→ Transferable Skills Identification→ Career Themes Developed→ Resolving Ambiguities→ Lifestyle Integration→ Monetary Needs Considerations→ Barriers to Success→ Identifying Perceived and Real Constraints

Opportunity Awareness

Collecting Appropriate Information→ Research → Organization Environments→ Community Information Gathering →Reality Testing →Networking →Mentoring→ Evaluating Results→ Career Action(s) Options Selection

Decision Learning

Evaluating Career Action Options→ Trade-offs→ Deciding on Goal→ Career Transition Scheduling

Transition Training

Rehearsing for Negotiations→ Developing Strategies for Success→ Checking Job-seeking Preparation→ Auditing Career Transition Progress

Transition Accomplished

Review of Completed Career Action Steps→ Assessment of Well-being→ New Learning Needs Diagnosed

▨ 5-SELF-ASSESSMENT ▨

Diagnosing the real problem

There can be many reasons for considering a change in your worklife.
It's important to isolate your particular reason or reasons, so that the
chosen alternative is not likely to cause a recurrence of them.
   Here is a checklist to assist you. Check where relevant to you.

☑ To avoid stress which is proving to be upsetting.

☑ Wish for a new lifestyle.

☐ Need for new stimulation following a personal trauma,
   such as relationship break-up, divorce or the death of a
   loved one.

☐ Desire to improve your knowledge and education. — *not specifically, tho am
   prepared to do this as the means
   to an end*

☐ New career options through increased availability of
   continuing education, technical change, economic shifts in
   demand and supply, fashion changes, etc.

☐ Laid off due to technological or organization change.

☑ Realization that your current career has limited prospects. / *opportunities for
   fulfillment*

☐ Significant change in your health.

☐ Change in your family's needs.

☑ Escape from monotonous occupation; need for a new
   challenge.

☐ Compulsory early retirement regulations in your current
   occupation.

☑ Preparation to relocate: city to country living, vice versa,
   overseas.   *means to an end
   again*

Audit Your Career Situation

Check the box if you agree with the question

☑ Do you carry a chip on your shoulder over some past ~~anger at U~~
setback to your career that could be obvious to ~~anger at self~~
others? *eg. potential new employer* ~~determination to seize it as an opportunity~~

☑ Are you made to feel like a second-class citizen where
you work?

☑ Do you behave self-consciously in front of senior
personnel where you work?

☐ Do you enjoy the company of your coworkers?

☑ Do you define your life in terms of both material and
intangible rewards not related to work?

☑ Are there problem areas at work that would interest
you as projects but are neglected by your employer?
~~eg real human issues eg. work dissatisfaction, m/ment training~~

☑ Does further advancement appear beyond your reach
for reasons that you cannot or will not control?

☐ Do you feel totally responsible for the way your
career is developing? ~~Should~~

☐ Have you identified an occupation(s) you might like to
try if your skills become obsolete where you work
now?

☐ Do you know the next logical step beyond your
current job which would clearly provide potential for
increased satisfaction and acquiring new skills?

☐ Have you assessed the most practical way to influence your boss to assist your career progress?

☐ Have you listed the apparent current constraints to
your career satisfaction?

☐ Is the financial security of your current salary package
inhibiting a change of career?

☐ Are you prepared for the next performance review
discussion with your boss (even though it may not yet
be scheduled)?

☐ Is the only important thing about the work you do the
pay you receive? ~~(giving notice)~~

Where are you right now?

Any time is a good time to examine what you are doing and why. In the process you can see more clearly how you come to make the decisions which affect your worklife; more importantly, you can use this data as a foundation to explore and decide where you need to be. Work through the following checklist — and be honest with yourself. Remember, you are the one who will benefit if you are.

Yes/No

Skills

Am I using my best and most enjoyed skills in my present job? ☐ ☑ *eg. versatility, enthusiasm*

Have I recently developed any new skills? .... ☑ ☐ *eg. awareness of political climate, what's needed to impress*

Have I improved some of the ones I had? ...... *eg: working thru others (in factory closure)* ☑ ☑ *only generically eg TM, maturity*

Do I know the skills I want to develop? .... ☐ ☑ *Some eg. confidence/ 79 assertiveness*

Am I doing something about it? .... ☐ ☑ *Not structured* **Self-assessment**

Do I know which of my skills are transferable to other jobs or occupations? .... ☑ ☐ *All, tho not nec'ly all at once*

~~Needs and values~~ .... ☐ ☐

Have I looked at my needs and values recently? .... ☐ ☑ *Redo Lifeplan*

Am I working towards satisfying as many as possible? .... ☐ ☐ *"*

Do some of them need clarification? .... ☑ ☐

Job

Is the job I have the one I really want? .... ☐ ☑

Am I working towards what I really want? .... ☐ ☑

Do I know all I need to know about the work which I want? ... ☐ ☑

Am I doing something about it? .... ☑ ☐

Goals

Do I have career goals for the next three years? .... ☐ ☑

Have I recently revised my life goals? .... ☐ ☑ ~~Lifeplan~~ *Longer term*

Am I consciously working towards them? .... ☐ ☑

	Yes/No

Have I reached any of my goals recently? .... ☑ ☐

Am I constantly evaluating my progress and rewarding
    myself for the results? .... ☐☑ ☐ *Not in structured way*

Problem solving

Do I use creative problem solving to solve my problems? .... ☐ ☑

Do I accept responsibility for what happens to me at work? .... ☑ ☐ *Now*

Do I believe that I can't always choose what happens to me,
    but I can choose the attitude I adopt towards it? .... ☑ ☐

Communication

Am I working towards improving my career
    development skills? .... ☑ ☐

Do I have a supportive group of friends who would
    encourage my career transition? .... ☐ ☑

Are my relationships with others at work improving? .... ☐ ☑

Learning from your experience
(job content analysis)

The following questions will encourage you to think about your
present or most recent job critically. Write down your answers to
each of the following:

[handwritten: Trying to base answers on last 2/2½ yrs]

- My main responsibilities are/were ... *[handwritten: Transition from Trainee to Mgr — swift progression — range of task areas — some people m/ment — meeting personal objectives]*
- Since I have been/while I was in the job it changed in these
ways... *[handwritten: Greater self-awareness of gap that had grown between my actual performance (real & perceived) and potential]*
- I enjoy(ed) the job for these reasons... *[handwritten: Overall remuneration; look on CV; good 'experience' at start of career]*
- I dislike(d) the job for these reasons... *[handwritten: Wrong environment; despised position got myself into & my own reactions; most of 'key players'; disliked politics; ideas on 'impressing the boss']*
- The job has developed the following new abilities in me... *[handwritten: dealing with politics; desire to find greater fulfilment, not another job; optimism; ideas on 'impressing the boss']*
- I am/was not acquiring the following new abilities ... *[handwritten: Job satisfaction; collaborating & building work relationships — relating to others]*

- I am/was not acquiring the following abilities which I believe I need for my future career... *(As above)* knowledge of a right fit; *Selling myself & Marketing anything /everything*
- This would be/have been a much better job if the following were/had been different... *(Like)/Respect colleagues; recognition of own* *performance or potential; stimulating + challenging environment; 'blend' with rest of life vice versa*
- In order to excel at the job I should have done/needed to do the following... *Learned better to keep head low /sell self at appropriate times /bide my time better by keeping a wider perspective of where I was*

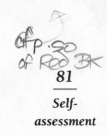

Reflection

Write about ten to fifteen lines summarizing the checklists you have just completed. Record the key issues you want to resolve. Place them in order of priority for your attention. By completing this summary you will isolate which factors deserve more attention than others in your quest for improvement in your worklife satisfaction.

Deficiency analysis (job content analysis)

The following exercise will highlight issues which concern you about your work activity. The questions are not intended to be a complete list, but prompters for your thinking about worklife issues. Write down your answers.

- You work because... *we all have to (money to fund lifestyle); social expectations; seek fulfilment of potential; significant part of overall lifestyle*
- When you are at work, what do you often wish? *I was elsewhere! Didn't feel as if I'm wasting time; enjoyment; was fulfilling potential; adding to my life in a positive frame of mind); was next step on 'ladder' of achievement /unclear*
- Success at your current work means...to you. *N/A (getting out cleanly + direction)*
- What is missing from your current worklife? *Link to rest of life; ability to succeed /feel good about self; good working r/ships*
- Do you need and/or want to develop some new area of skill? What specifically?

? 'Specialism', or at least chance to do justice to interest areas
Work r/ships
Influencing others
Marketing self/anything
Improved Communications (the key) to all

- Do you need more knowledge of a particular work-related subject? Which? *All knowledge is good if learning can be applied at a later date. Will need knowledge of alternative career areas*
- How much of your skill and knowledge is being used in your current work? *? A lot more would be if I were committed to it ie. if potential were being released*
- How do you feel about the amount of work that you have? *Volume ok usually; recognition that interesting work would probably be more time-consuming as would put more of myself into it*
- Are you restricted by the confines of your current job description? *expectations — Yes*

- Do you have problems keeping up-to-date in your area of specialty? *No, altho willpower is not there to maintain a wider knowledge-base*
- What are the behavioral and personal characteristics of your boss that are causing a reduction in your efficiency? *Undue Unwillingness to spend necy time to effect a change; self-centredness; task-orientation*
- With what kinds of people do you work ineffectively at present? *Largely upwards, tho much room for improvement with peer group and especially 'subordinates'*
- Do you feel the need to relinquish some of your responsibilities? *No*

- What have you tried to avoid doing at work in the past week? *Creating more workload; having actual Confrontation*

Objectives analysis (skills search)

A key factor in the development of your career is the striving for particular objectives. You established many of these objectives for yourself. You would also have been working towards objectives set by others — parents, partners or former supervisors or a combination of yours and theirs. The distinction was probably unclear. Past experiences in relation to these objectives have to some degree either increased or decreased your self-esteem and personal satisfaction.

One thing you can be sure of is that while you have been striving to achieve certain objectives, you have developed new skills or improved existing ones. Failure, as well as success, has already taught you much about yourself. Past failure is of particular value if you take the time now to explore what objectives were involved and why it occurred.

Step 1:   Record as many of the objectives as you can remember in your life from your mid-teens to today. Write down

cf reverse of P-15?

what other people expected of you. Then add those objectives you set for yourself. Whether they were all accomplished is not important at this stage.

Step 2: Record what actually happened while working towards each objective.

Step 3: You now have a goldmine of information where close examination will reveal the skills you used. Write them down quickly as they occur to you as you read what you have recorded. It may be useful to refer to page 55 where a useful series of definitions of skills is provided. You may have been thinking you don't have much to offer. Just look at the length of your new inventory of skills!

Step 4: Score each of the identified skills you know you have. Your own data proved to you that they exist. First, assign a rating out of 10 (regarding 10 as high) for your aptitude for them or capability for using them. Second, give a separate rating out of 10 for those which, on reflection, you actually gained satisfaction from using.

Step 5: Transfer the two sets of ratings onto another page, but only those skills which have been rated highest by you. Take a cut-off point — say 7 out of 10 — to facilitate your selection for transfer to the new list.

There before you are the skills you would be wise to use in future work activity in order to achieve a higher level of personal well-being.

If you have become stuck with this exercise and your second attempt has not secured a breakthrough, then do the next exercise as an alternative.

Achievement analysis (skills search) cf reverse p. 151

A method of identifying the skills you have and enjoy using is to identify and analyze your achievements.

Write down a list of achievements in your life since leaving school — you should find at least twelve. The achievements listed should reveal what you enjoyed doing. Some of them may not have been acknowledged by others but that doesn't matter. What *you* think you have accomplished is important. Your achievements should come from both your worklife and areas of your past activities outside employment.

If you have difficulty recalling all your achievements from many years of living, take each three or five year period of your life since age eighteen. Examine each period in turn. This will trigger your recall of the achievements. You are likely to be surprised at the nature and number of your successes. Listing many of your earlier achievements in different spheres of your life gives an important boost to self-esteem.

Your opinion is important here — not the opinion of your previous supervisor, manager, parent(s) or friends. In fact, you are likely to write down several achievements which other people did not know about. They may include a procedure you improved, a money-saving idea you developed or completing a particular course of study — at this stage, the nature of the achievement is not as important as how you feel about the achievement when you think about it now.

Use the following to jog your memory and help you find evidence of your capabilities when recording and analyzing your achievements:

- Specific instances when you saved your employer money.

- Examples of when you increased sales, exceeded quotas or successfully introduced a new product or service.

- Ideas and proposals you submitted which were subsequently adopted by your employer.

- Any major projects in which you had responsibility or led the activity.

- Any procedures, policies, programs or changes that you introduced which were successful and solved problems.

- Events or situations in which your involvement was viewed positively by those around you.

Now examine each achievement and write down the skills you used to accomplish it. If you find you're having problems identifying skills for your statements of achievement, refer to page 56 for definitions of what is a skill.

Use the following action verbs to start your sentences:

accelerated	accomplished	administered
analyzed	arranged	awarded
budgeted	built	calculated
communicated	completed	composed
conceived	conducted	controlled
coordinated	counselled	created
decreased	delivered	demonstrated
designed	developed	devised
directed	edited	eliminated
established	estimated	evaluated
expanded	expedited	founded
generated	guided	implemented
improved	increased	initiated
instituted	instructed	interviewed
invented	launched	led
maintained	managed	maximized
modified	monitored	motivated
negotiated	optimized	organized
originated	performed	persuaded
planned	prepared	produced
proved	provided	publicized
rationalized	reduced	researched
reviewed	revised	saved
scheduled	selected	sold
solved	streamlined	structured
supervised	taught	trained
	won	

Each skill identified is an important clue to your future well-being. Later you will discard those skills you don't enjoy using. Most of the skills you enjoy using should be components of your next job — whether with your current employer or elsewhere. It's logical that you are more likely to enjoy job tasks that involve the skills you enjoy using.

Behavior analysis
(employment environment analysis)

What happens to us at work is very much related to how others react to our appearance and behavior in different situations. How others see us helps them decide how to react to us. So our feelings about our well-being at work are intimately bound up with issues involving colleagues, whether subordinates, coworkers or supervisors.

To analyze how we appear to others is very important. What each one of us does with our reflections on our behavior and its effect on others is something only we can decide. The insight we gain from this analysis may inspire a decision to change the types of people with whom we prefer to work.

Step 1: Write about aspects of your personality which you feel should be taken into account in any work situation. Add comments about the way you dress, speak and behave.

Step 2: Write about the same number of words on another page describing the way you think you appear to others. Think of several events which have occurred recently at work and record what you believe other people thought about your actions.

Step 3: It's not easy to see ourselves as we think others see us. Asking another person to help can be useful. Show both pages to one of your colleagues and ask for their views on what you have written. Think deeply about any differences between their comments and what you have written. With their help you have identified important clues to what aspects of your behavior may be having a detrimental effect on your worklife satisfaction and/or

86

*Career
Analysis
and Life
Management
Planning*

career progress. It also tests how closely your image of yourself matches the image of you held by others.

Step 4:   Now, make a list of those aspects identified as contributing little to your work satisfaction. Then mark those which you now know must be changed before you can realistically expect an improvement in your degree of satisfaction at work, whether you stay in your current occupation with the same employer or change one or both.

Step 5:   Specify the characteristics of people who, by your contact with them, bring out the behavior with which you are most comfortable in your conduct at work. It's important to document your opinions as to what type of people you would prefer to interact with.

Lively; preferably young; stimulating; living life; competent; flexible & dynamic;

Step 6:   With the new insights you have acquired so far in this exercise, describe the job tasks that would appear to be a good fit with your personality. Don't worry if you do not know at this stage what occupational title applies to your description. That will be found later.

87

Self-assessment

Event analysis (employment environment analysis)

The work you currently carry out may not include the best mix of job tasks for you. On the other hand, you may consider it does, but would feel reassured if this were confirmed in some way.

This exercise requires you to trace the events that brought you to your current type of job tasks and to examine your feelings about these in retrospect. In this search there may be clues that contribute to the decision to remain in your current occupation or seek a change.

A further benefit of your work on event analysis will be the use of the data later in this book when you are shown how to plan your career. When planning your career action steps later on, the outcome of this work will help you make effective use of these events.

When you reflect on your employment experiences and career to date, certain events probably stand out — events that may have led to a change in your approach to your work and/or life management.

① I/viewing in Dublin & UK for Fords — challenge of early responsibilities; application of self to new situations; acceptance of competence by others

② Work r/ship v. AIG — you lose if you don't manage a satisfactory outcome / can seriously affect whole life & bring out awful, destructive side

③ Factory closure — perspectives; closer access to aims of org'ns, comparitive values etc.

Step 1:	Identify at least three key events that you know made a difference within you and in your behavior at work. Write what happened and what you learned from the event and whether you experienced a good, or not so good, outcome.
Step 2:	Learning from the past is not looking back with regrets, but rather interpreting the positive aspects which may provide important clues to your next career action step. The effect may have been either brief or long-lasting. Look over the questions which follow and write more about yourself as you feel you are prompted:

Your future is yours

1st reaction — no-one stands out; is this because **88** of weak r/ships or because —— tend to sponge from wide range of people?

Career Analysis and Life Management Planning

AIG instead of drop to — personalised it; avoided confronting; allowed self-esteem lending deteriorating performance — downward spiral

Soups project (which turned out to be nothing more than a project)

1st reaction — 'scary' not correct word; as in most intense sit'ns (e.g. AIG appraisal, closure ① etc) strong emotions (anger; excitement/confidence) presided; loss NP i/view after threw Bewalls job — fighting for survival

Cynical; s/times bitter; less motivated & keen/jovial Also, matured & better using r/ships. Instant recognition of 'fit' with own wants/abilities

Manage them/before they (mismanage you) to your possible detriment *successfully*

- What is the most significant thing you have learned from your employment life which you would pass onto someone else?
- Describe the person who has taught you best during your career. This may be in relation to your work tasks or personal behavior.
- What has been your most significant interpersonal conflict at work? Why was the situation difficult in your relations with the other person?
- What work event situation did you take very seriously at the time, but are able to laugh about now?
- Describe the most scary situation you have tackled during your career so far — one you had to handle which caused you apprehension.
- If you met a person today who knew you at work several years ago, in what ways would they say you have changed?
- Though you may have been encouraged by positive comments from others, what caused you to realize that you would succeed in a particular work-related endeavor?
- What did you learn from working for the person you least liked during your career to date?

Step 3: Review your writings thoroughly. Look for a pattern in the very private, personal statements you have made. At the very least, you should find many clues about situations to avoid in the future which threaten your sense of well-being and inhibit progress in your career.

The bonus may be data which confirms that you should stay in your current occupation, but change your employer; or change your occupation with either your current employer or an alternative employer. There is a lot more to learn as well. Think hard. Revisit your writings on several occasions, at a time and a place where you can be free from distractions.

Step 4: Does what you have written, read, thought about and read again amend a career action step you have in mind? Write in what way.

Enjoyment factors (employment environment analysis)

Write the following headings at the top of four separate pages:

1 **Job, hobby, voluntary tasks, sports**

2 **What was achieved?**

3 **Results and recognition received?**

4 **What aspects did I enjoy most?**

Now, start writing — don't worry about writing your notes in the date order they occurred. Go back into your past as far as you like. Leave out any job or employment period you wish to forget. Think of the activities which you have told your partner or special friend and those you have met periodically at social gatherings. It's not important at this stage what relevance your notes have to any new occupation or career

Notice that you are asked to include not only jobs as an employee but other activities in which you have demonstrated some skill and acquired experience. Go back far into your past. The clues to your career direction problem may well be in an activity you engaged in many years ago.

The apparent size of the achievement is not very important. Achievements may be those recognized in some way by others or they may be ones of which only you are aware. Don't be too modest. Nobody else is going to see your notes unless you want them to. Look for examples that prove you did a good job whatever the activity.

Measure each activity in terms of amount of time spent, money earned, awards/bonuses earned, benefits to others. Record these points on the "Results and recognition received" page. Include prizes, commendations, election to committees, published articles, new business orders received and any factual detail which illustrates your success.

The page "What aspects I enjoyed most?" is particularly important. Take for example "meeting or working with people". It's likely you have entered this on page four. Analyze what you really enjoyed. Ask yourself questions such as: Was it being involved with groups or individuals? What kind of people did you like to interview, meet or teach? What exactly did occur to cause this feeling of satisfaction?

This is a time-consuming exercise. You may need to rewrite your notes several times. It could be beneficial to take several breaks — perhaps start again on another day.

When you are satisfied that you have a complete list, check for a pattern. It may take time to spot but one will be there in your notes. See what recurs most often in the activities you have listed. The pattern will be the signpost to what you really want to be included in your next career action.

Your next career should include at least some of the enjoyment areas which you have listed. If it doesn't, you are probably heading in the wrong direction. To like the work in your next career action, you will really have to want to do it. Otherwise, it will be difficult to write job applications and convince prospective employers of your value, let alone achieve success in the occupation. There is nothing more likely to succeed in a job interview than your real conviction about what you want to do.

Your personal wants (lifestyle analysis)

Where will tomorrow find you? Will you be working in a job you like and perform well? The following activity is designed to help you think through what it is what you want from a job.

Knowing what you want is, of course, essential for decision making about alternative career directions, but it also makes it possible to communicate clearly to those who might be able to help you.

Most people view job assignments as a means of satisfying personal wants to some degree. Listed below are personal wants which might be satisfied through next steps such as future job assignments, professional development actions or change in your current job. In your next career step what do you want?

[handwritten, right margin: NB.]
[handwritten: DONE THINKING OF 1ST 'CONSOLIDATION' JOB IN OZ]

Step 1:   Select the eight personal wants in the list which follows that are most important to you in your next job and underline them.

Geographical location   *[handwritten: Right part of Sydney; near home (beach / parkland / centre)]*

Enjoyment   *[handwritten: Atmosphere; colleagues; blend into rest of the]*

Self-realization

Social service

×Prestige

Morality

×High salary

Travel

People-centered position   *[handwritten: Integral]*

Good hours

Opportunities for physical activity

Lack of pressure

Physical challenge

Excitement

Intellectual work

Creativity   *[handwritten: Inspired daily]*

×Fringe benefits ×

×Opportunities for advancement×

Security

×Supervision responsibilities

Pleasant work conditions

Meaningful work

×Psychic satisfaction ×

Variety of work

Opportunity to solve problems
x Compassionate boss or supervisor
Self-supervision   ie. Flexibility
Leadership opportunities
Feeling of group affiliation
Tangible achievement
x Contribution to organization x
Opportunity for continuous learning
x Hygienic and modern facilities: office, lounge,
    cafeteria, etc. x
x Personal power x
Fun work
More free time
Money   Sufficient for current lifestyle/
Independence   future plans
x Professional status x
Challenge
Freedom from worry
Friends (eg. initially) from work + subsequent contacts
Cultural opportunities
Recreation
x Visibility
Climate / work environment   All of above
x Educational facilities x
x Leadership
More time with family

Step 2:   Select the eight personal wants which are least important to you in your next career step and draw a line
through them.

Step 3:   Does your present job setting offer possibilities for sat-
N/A   isfying what you want most in your next step?
If yes, describe how. If no, what environment is
indicated?

Step 4:   Do you want your next job assignment to satisfy your
eight most important wants? If yes, how? If no, why?

Step 5:   Do you need to develop some new skills or abilities to improve your potential for achieving your eight most important wants in your next step? If so, what skills or abilities should you develop in preparation?

Choice of area
" " worktype
" " firm

Step 6:   Can or must some of your wants be satisfied off the job? If so, what does this mean in terms of how you would consider any future positions?

Step 7:   Summarize what you personally want and what you can and will do to satisfy the wants you have selected.

put up with s'thing temporary while I cast around

Step 8:   Consider reviewing this exercise with your partner or a close friend.

Lifestyle fit

Another way to evaluate your preferred lifestyle fit with your job content is to compete the following questions defining what you really want:

- I am living in (city, country town, rural) ...

- I would like to live in... *presumably... a flat, comfortable place in London*

- I work in (office, shop, outdoors, etc)... *quite variety*

- I would like to work in...

- In my time outside work I now...

- In my time outside work I would like to...

- My current hours at work are...

- I would like my working hours to be...

Your fantasy analysis

During our journey through life each of us has dreamt about what we would like to be and to do. Time, money, self-confidence, motivation and other factors have blunted these ambitions and they have been discarded, "parked" or been suppressed.

A considered study of these dreams or occupational fantasies can produce a list of: (a) barriers to their fulfillment; and (b) your personal strengths. You will often find, in the process of the study, that your strengths outweigh these barriers and an exciting career transition can, in fact, follow. Your fantasy can become a reality. It is worthwhile to undertake this form of study.

There are several ways to tap into your fantasies. One is to finish the sentence "My almost impossible dream is ...". Another is to write down your response to "If you had your choice of all things to do, present constraints notwithstanding, what would you do?" Your self-analysis work using this method will uncover significant wishes and values, some of which have been long buried in the process of living.

What was your original dream? It may sound impossible to achieve now but stated in different terms your dream may well become possible. Experiment writing your dreams this way.

Occupational fantasies expand your awareness of job possibilities beyond the conventional. When your fantasy is written down, put it through a number of reality checks which are described in Chapter 7. It may well emerge that you can do what you really want to do!

Reread and, if you wish, record your feelings as you read over your writings. Consider the fact that how much you want something does affect whether or not you achieve it. Answer the following questions:

- What would I gain most from achieving this fantasy?

- What restrains me from making this change?

- What would be the worst thing that could happen if I made the change that I have described? If this happened, what could I do?

- If I really wanted to implement this fantasy, what would be my first step? my second? my third?

Your biographical review

The career analysis technique of biographical review is very thorough. It is a well proven method of moving to greater self-awareness, expanding creativity and providing a focus for making important decisions. The process of writing down an account of all your worklife experiences provides you with a great deal of personal power. It is, in effect, a retrospective diary.

Through your biographical review you will become aware of how you have been changing and growing, moving through phases and crossroads and the effect all this has on your current outlook. A new sense of confidence should develop which is necessary before you proceed to think through and find creative solutions to your worklife concerns.

Many people have commented to me that writing a biographical review is getting in touch with their inner self. As you record your experiences you can check your earlier decisions and evaluate our feelings about people, situations and employment environments.

Your biographical writings are likely to begin tentatively and self-consciously. As you experiment with different styles of recording you will become more comfortable and words will soon come faster than you can write them down. It is a safe place to record what you think about yourself, your work and the events that have been significant in your journey to date through life.

Remember that you give power to whatever you focus on when writing, so concentrate on the happier moments of you worklife experiences and do not dwell long on the negative. Take frequent breaks from the task but do not procrastinate about returning to it as your biographical review is a powerful means of realizing your own true potential.

You need to be prepared to work very hard. This exercise takes considerable time. There will be times when you are tempted to skip over a step or to complete one less than conscientiously. You will find it best to establish a steady pace of so much writing time per day, so many hours per week. The value to you will be very much affected by how much time, effort and self-honesty you devote to each step of the process.

A thorough written account of your past will help you identify skills and capabilities that have been lost in the crowded detail of your past.

Write about all your work experiences. Include part-time and casual jobs, work you did while at school, during college and while searching for full-time employment. Move on to examine and write about all the jobs which followed — position by position. Start with your first job and conclude with your current or most recent employment.

Remember, it is not simply a chronological history of your employment dates. It is a comprehensive written expression of your recollection of likes and dislikes in all aspects of your worklife. Your opinions, feelings and conclusions must be recorded before your data can be profitably used to help make worklife planning decisions.

Your biographical review requires you to look backward and trace the elements, happenings and people who have influenced your life's journey so far. It is understanding the positives and negatives that helps you to appraise the wealth and value of your experiences.

The employment history part of your biography should include:

- details of what you actually did. Job titles and dates of employment are simply not enough. List your job tasks, your responsibilities, etc.;

- an account of the good and not so good features of your work. Let yourself really go to town here. This is a private record, so write down your feelings about these features: activities, accomplishments, the types of people you worked with, etc.;

- a description of each of the employment environments in which you have worked (size, number of people you supervised, industry, ethics, state of morale among other staff, your feelings at the time);

- an account of any position in volunteer and/or community service activities;

- a record of features, such as hard work, taking chances, making trade-offs and good friends;

- your description of any indecision, envy, setbacks and disappointments. Understanding both positive and negative events helps make change possible in your next career action.

It's not the time to be humble, reticent or shy — write down what you think you contributed to your work environment. Be as thorough over the earlier employment experiences as with the more recent and easier to remember — the clues to future work contentment might well be there.

Now the worst news. You have not done a really thorough job unless your descriptions cover at least thirty pages! If they don't, go back again over each job or important nonwork event in your adult life and write more. This exercise is very hard work, so take time to complete it, two or three weeks if necessary.

If possible, type or write your data double-spaced with wide margins. This will facilitate the work you do in Chapter 6 with the information.

▓ 6-Interpreting Data ▓

F inding the answers to what we want to do requires us to search for signs amidst the data our self-assessment has accumulated. Once we have identified the stars, just as navigators do, we will have our bearings. When we have our bearings we can develop a strategy to arrive at where we have discovered we want to be. Identifying the stars is the purpose of the following exercises associated with interpreting data.

Classifying your skills

Identifying and classifying your skills and capabilities into groups — each with a common theme — is a critical step towards identifying those worklife activities in which you are most likely to perform well and achieve satisfaction. Just to sit and think about all we know about work procedures, business techniques and organizational life is not a reliable way of identifying the whole extent of our knowledge. We accumulate knowledge rapidly. Our ability to recall and sort this data accurately does not match the efficiency of a computer. Yet the search for the sum of our knowledge and to identify what parts of that knowledge we like using are critical parts of the quest for well-being at work. The thoroughness with which you carry out this exercise will contribute to:

- greater accuracy in selecting the most appropriate career action step, operating level and type of environment in which to advance your career.

- an increase in your confidence and ability to convince selection panels, managers or interviewers of your suitability and strength of motivation to perform the tasks of the next job you aim to secure.

Remind yourself during this research that an important aspect of career analysis is directed at identifying tasks where you used the skills you have discovered you really have and enjoy using. The easiest trap is to look only at past job titles rather than the tasks and skills behind them. It is the tasks performed and skills used rather than the job title which provide or negate satisfaction in worklife.

- Every job, whatever its title, is made up of a set of tasks. Each of these tasks requires a number of skills. Your first activity is to identify all your skills by examining all the tasks you have carried out, then those skills you most like using.

- Remember: skills are action-oriented words or statements which describe the function you were carrying out, such as public speaking, computing figures, organizing others, etc.

- Capabilities are personal traits like perseverance, honesty, etc. which describe the manner in which you applied these skills. Here are some examples: deeply concerned, enjoyed the challenge, earned respect, built a good team.

- Your search for these skills is for any evidence of ability, natural competence, proficiency or personal quality you have demonstrated.

Step 1:   Skills Assembly

Find your skills and capabilities using the following as a guide:

- Look over your responses to all the self-assessment exercises in Chapter 5 to detect and write down your total list of skills, such as ability, writing, training/teaching others, etc.

- Reread every line, every sentence. Add to your list as additional skills reveal themselves.

- Be wary of using generalized terms such as financial management: Was the skill used actually cost analysis, budget planning or capital expenditure evaluations?

- Take several days over this exercise to allow your thoughts to crystalize. Aim to have a list of seventy skills within five days of beginning this analysis.

Remind yourself repeatedly that skills are action-oriented words or statements. Personal qualities or

100

*Career
Analysis
and Life
Management
Planning*

capabilities are traits which characterize a person. Skills, for which you are searching, may be one word descriptions or short sentences.

Step 2:   Skills Classification

- Go back over your list of skills. Classify each skill by listing it under the particular skill most allied to it. Cross out from your original list as you transfer each one. New major skill headings or classifications will occur as you do this.

- Don't be concerned about listing a skill under more than one classification heading. This is likely to happen quite often.

Step 3:   Skills Rating

- When all your skills and capabilities have been transferred to the new classifications, take each group in turn and read down each classification and mark with a three (3) skills you know well and enjoy/enjoyed using. Put a two (2) for skills you know well, but do not or did not enjoy very much. Put a one (1) against those skills which you currently know little about using, but would like to know more.

- Put each classified group in order of preference by listing them according to the number of threes (3s) you have rated the skills within each group. You will arrive at a point where you are very much wiser about whether a career direction change is suggested and which occupations best suit your skills. It should be a pleasant surprise to know that each group is, in fact, a separate occupation — a new career — plus is the proof that you can carry out the tasks involved within each one identified. At the same time you have assembled the data essential for an effective job search or promotion claim. The data can be used in a new resume, job application letters, face-to-face selection interviews, performance review discussions or career planning reviews with your manager.

Step 4:   Review

- Go back over your total self-search responses. Yes, one more time. The intention is to extract from them every single skill and capability that you have ever used and demonstrated. The more thoroughly you do this search, the more you will discover your personal uniqueness. And, therefore, the easier you will identify the most appropriate work content for you.

- You may need the help of another person to uncover all the skills. If you feel that you are stuck but believe more can be found, recruit a friend to review your data.

You may feel at this stage that all this hard work is not worth the effort. You are probably thinking that you will have to take whatever jobs are available in employment environments and locations far from your ideal choice.

There can, of course, be no watertight promise that you will find a career direction exactly suiting the new worklife objectives you are developing from this. Nevertheless, do persevere — there are several reasons why you should:

- You will feel more confident as a result of identifying your real strengths and desires. This will make the search for new worklife conditions less of a strain on your emotions, as this self-confidence will be noticed by others.

- You may need to learn that there are many hidden job opportunities in every location and several promotion-seeking or job search techniques, not generally known, which may help to obtain one of them

- Once you have thoroughly identified your ideal job content, employment environment and lifestyle preference, you will feel a renewed motivation and feeling of self-management that will bring about substantial results. This renewed motivation and self-confidence will enable you to surmount many obstacles in reaching your goals. But it's not just your attitude which influences your likely success. These exercises will produce convincing evidence of the wisdom of your new direction, and

102

*Career
Analysis
and Life
Management
Planning*

the critical evidence you can use to persuade people with the authority to promote, transfer or hire you.

Another benefit from persevering with this hard work is the realization of just how much information you have assembled about yourself. When you have reached this stage you have accomplished more than most people ever do. I'm sure you were already aware of much of the information you have assembled, but I'm confident that you have identified much more about yourself through these techniques of recall of past events. To consolidate "old" and "new" information is a very special achievement.

Gender Bias — Not Theirs, But Yours!

How has your view of what is appropriate for your
    sex influenced your career path?

In what ways has your sex:
    contributed to or interfered with your career
      achievements?
    affected your feelings of career success?

Your inner and outer constraints

This exercise will help you interpret the inner and outer constraints which affect your career choices and may be perceived as obstacles in the way of your quest for worklife satisfaction.

Documenting and reviewing your perceived constraints helps develop a more accurate career direction because it includes dealing with nonwork elements that nevertheless affect your worklife. Your hopes and aspirations are affected by the inhibitions and/or constraints in your personal circumstances. Yet I have noticed many times in worklife counselling that when perceived constraints have been written down, the individual has been able to separate the real constraints from those that are imagined. What at first was viewed as an obstacle can, on reflection, be reduced substantially and, sometimes, even removed.

Reflect on your life and current situation. Consider the constraints which follow and complete each sentence.

- My health constrains my career in the following ways...

- The health of a family member constrains my career in the following ways...

- My education constrains my career as follows...

- My origins and upbringing constrain my career in the following ways...

- My spiritual beliefs constrain my career in the following ways...

- My age constrains my career in the following ways...

- My physical self constrains my career in the following ways...

- My commitments (financial, emotional, etc.) constrain my career in the following ways....

- My view of myself (self-concept) constrains my career in the following ways...

- My geographical location constrains my career in the following ways...

- My current employment environment constrains my career in the following ways...

- My opinion of other people's prejudices towards me and/or what I currently do constrains my career in the following ways...

What steps could you take to counteract the constraints that could influence you to settle for unsatisfying work?

Example of Constraints

I've done well in my career considering I haven't had education beyond secondary school. That didn't matter in the past but now there are many in the company with degrees and even post-graduate qualifications. I've got the impression I'm not being considered for further promotion because I don't have a college education. Is it too late to do something about this?

Example of Constraints

I've been with the same firm for almost twelve years. Friends and business associates seem to think this is too long to stay with one employer. I'm confused about what to do and wonder what the options are for me at my age.

Meeting other people's expectations

In career analysis it is important to identify to what degree you have absorbed the expectations of others.

- Who influences your values and self-concept and by how much?

- Who are the significant people in your life and what do they expect of you in terms of your career?

We frequently mirror others' requirements of us. There is a danger that we may take this a stage further and do in our career actions what others expect or appear to demand of us. Acting a part rather than being our real self can take over. We can consequently take the "wrong" turn in our career because we have not considered our choices in our own terms or deeply enough.

This exercise will help you to clarify your self-concept by identifying what others want you to be, to do or to think. This will help to identify **what you really want** and expect from yourself. Once completed, it will be easier to determine what is your own thinking and what is inherited from others and needs to be identified as such.

- In each of the six blocks record the name of the person who fits the description.

- Record at least three expectations you believe each person such as mother, boss, etc. wanted you or wants you now to value. Complete each box except **Me** before the next step.

- Underline each expectation that you also want for yourself.

- Transfer the underlined expectations into the circle headed **Me**.

- Review the implications of your recordings; consider with

whom it could be useful to share your analysis of their expectations and yours, particularly where they differ.

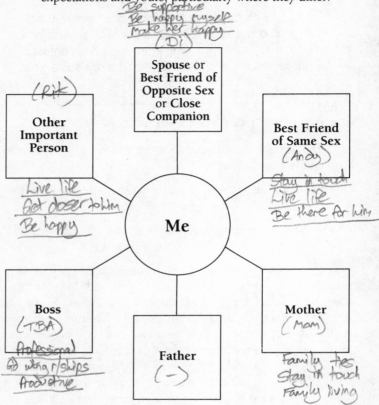

Be supportive
Be happy myself
make her happy
(Di)

(Rik)

Other Important Person

Live life
Get closer to him
Be happy

Spouse or
Best Friend of Opposite Sex or Close Companion

Me

Best Friend of Same Sex
(Andy)

Stay in touch
Live life
Be there for him

Boss
(TBA)

Professional
Go wking r/ships
Productive

Father
(-)

Mother
(Mam)

Family ties
Stay in touch
Family living

Meeting Other People's Expectations Chart

Reflection

Write what you think the people you are close to believe is the role of work in their lives. Comment on how you differ in this regard.

Time allocation analysis

On the following page are two diagrams representing the 24-hour clock. By comparing what actually happens in your current routine with what you would like to happen, important information will emerge to contribute to the realistic career planning you will be undertaking shortly.

Add the hours 1 to 12 twice to the diagrams. Using different colors, shade in your current time allocation for the following activities on your average weekday. Repeat on the second diagram, but enter the amount of time you would prefer to allocate over the next twelve months in order to bring about a more desirable balance of activities in your life.

- With family
- With friends
- At work
- Doing chores for yourself and/or others
- Alone (time spent reflecting on events, situations, relationships, the future)
- Educational activities/college education course, etc.
- Pursuing hobbies
- Asleep
- Commuting/travelling
- Relaxation, reading, watching television, etc. (staying still!)
- Sporting activities

Review the complete diagrams and record your responses to:

- Am I satisfied with the manner in which my time is spent at present?
- What obstacles need to be overcome in order to alter this allocation to bring about increased personal satisfaction and self-worth?
- How often do I see my parents or other relatives? How important are these meetings to me?
- Who else do I see regularly for social companionship? How much would I miss these meetings?
- What are my family obligations which restrict the hours I could work (and study, if necessary)?

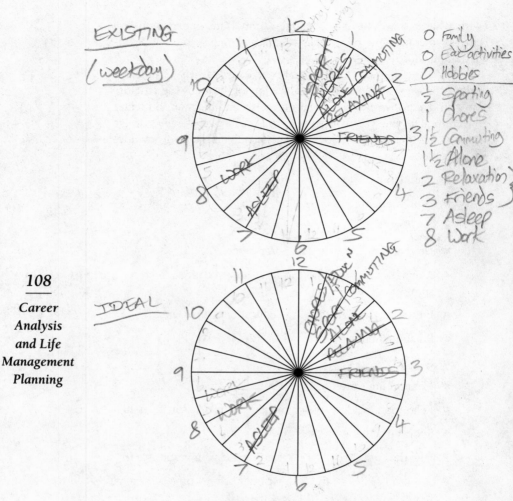

EXISTING
(weekday)

IDEAL

0	Family
0	Edu. activities
0	Hobbies
½	Sporting
1	Chores
3½	Commuting
1½	Alone
2	Relaxation
3	Friends
7	Asleep
8	Work

Time Allocation Analysis Charts

Thinking ahead

Your analysis in Chapter 5 will have helped you decide those worklife features you would like to have and those you would be quite happy not to experience again. So often we concentrate on the current incidents in our worklife situation rather than on being in a new place or situation.

108

*Career
Analysis
and Life
Management
Planning*

The next three exercises are called visualization — a method of raising our motivation to move forward and accomplish a specific goal. It should also help you improve your focus on your new realistic career and worklife objectives. As you proceed, think of all the new information about yourself that has surfaced so far. Incorporate much of it into what you write now.

Picture yourself two years from today. Conjure up the desired activities for a complete week. In other words, start on a Sunday and describe in writing the desired activities on every day through to Saturday evening, encompassing both your work and personal life. Creating a convincing picture in words of where you would like to be two years from now will give a boost to your confidence that your next career action step will be successful and bring about desired results.

Your ideal job (1)

Assume that in two years' time you will receive a letter inviting you to apply for your ideal job. Your task now is to draft the letter you would like to receive. The following items must be included in your letter: title, salary range, type of business or industry, description of and expectations about things to be accomplished, the five most important requirements of the person to do the job and the geographical area in which the job is located. Additional information may be included as you wish. Take a break for about an hour and then return to the letter you have written. Now write your answers to the following:

- Are you ready to perform your ideal job now?

- If not, what do you need to do that is within your control to get ready?

- If you are ready now, what are you doing about it?

- Do you really enjoy doing the things most required by this job?

- What values in your life might be satisfied? compromised?

- Would your ideal job cause you to pretend to be what others want you to be or a reflection of your true self?

- Is your ideal job simply an unrealizable dream or is it really something which you can obtain?

- What would you change in your life, if anything, to increase your chances of obtaining the job you have described in two years' time?

- Did you discuss this exercise with your partner or close friend and what reaction did this person have to your writings?

Example of interpretation of data

written after completing several career analysis exercises. The writer had been abruptly laid off and, after suffering depression, set out with determination to reduce the likelihood of a recurrence.

During the past three weeks I have thought about who I am, what I like and dislike, what makes me happy and unhappy, when I am comfortable and uncomfortable and what I want to do with my life. I do not believe that I will ever come to firm conclusions since I am constantly changing. That is the nature of human life. But some things are relatively static and I have identified through career analysis some definite preferences.

I want to work in a people-oriented task environment in which I can avoid technically-oriented procedures. This partially limits my career options and excludes careers which are numbers-oriented or highly analytical. I am not inclined to pursue a career in accounting, finance or computer science. Instead, I consider line management, consulting or personnel as viable alternatives. I have never really considered marketing deeply. My educational training in marketing is limited. Furthermore, when I think of marketing I picture the highly ambitious manager who is constantly monitoring the activities of both colleagues and competitors to make sure he or she is one step ahead at all times. I envisage a successful marketeer as having deceived the public, something which is contrary to my values.

I enjoy interacting with people in a helping mode. I am concerned with getting along with others and I am influenced by them in my decision making. Although I realize that my characterization of a marketing professional is a stereotype, I believe these qualities were instrumental in my dissatisfaction with my career in this field of business.

110

*Career
Analysis
and Life
Management
Planning*

Line management is a viable career alternative. But I am eliminating it from consideration at this time. On the positive side, I evaluate a career in line management as providing the interactive environment I desire. It would give me a change to assume responsibility as well as the opportunity to motivate others. On the other hand, line management also means maintaining an operation in a line environment. This would require such activities as developing budgets, maintaining equipment and forecasting future needs. The people side of such a job is consistent with my self-assessment, but the equally important operation side deviates from my main preferences.

Management consulting is another option I am currently eliminating. As such, I would be analyzing management and business problems. This would allow me to be actively involved in decision making and planning which is consistent with my enjoyment of responsibility and setting and achieving high work standards. These factors seem to indicate a good fit but I need to find out more through research interviews. A good consultant is a confident decision maker and able to confront others easily and sell ideas.

I am not that self-assured. While a consultant interacts with people in a helping fashion, much of the work is individual and project-oriented. Affiliations with other people would play a subordinate role in responsibilities of this type of work. My research interviews to be undertaken may confirm my impression that a consultant functions in a relatively unstructured environment and usually works on several projects simultaneously. These characteristics would be inconsistent with my recent self-assessment deliberations. I have identified that I really prefer structured and organized activities.

My preliminary conclusion is that I could suit a career in personnel management.

I know now that I enjoy affiliation with other people yet appreciate the need for good commercial practices, as staff are such an expensive resource for a firm.

The need to cope with fast moving circumstances appeals to me. I enjoy a busy schedule, but if I am going to be really effective I will need to remind myself that I sometimes resist change. Well, my preliminary conclusion has been made. A rest before I tackle the next step, i.e. to check out what fits the profile I have evolved for myself.

Your ideal job (2)

Another way of undertaking the above exercise is to write your responses to the following statement:

"On this day two years hence the following differences in my worklife will be apparent..."

Reflection on completion of Chapter 6

What do you now know about who you are? Complete each of the following two lists:

I am this..   I am not this...

112

*Career
Analysis
and Life
Management
Planning*

■ 7-OPPORTUNITY ■ AWARENESS

Self-help group analysis

Career analysis is very hard work. Because you are looking at yourself intently during the self-assessment and interpreting data exercises there is a danger of being too severe in the analysis of who you are and what you can offer. Everyone differs in their ability to take a systematic approach to sorting through complex personal issues. It is not hard to find another person who is also worried about a lack of career or life management satisfaction. In fact, a poll of your friends and acquaintances is likely to reveal many who are deeply concerned, but unsure what to do about it.

The creation of a self-help group is a very practical step. Limit the group size to five. Try to have members in the group from different occupational backgrounds but with ages no more than eight years apart.

Step 1:   Homework must be done before the self-help group meets. A written record of what each has done in their career to date must be prepared. An up-to-date resume would serve this purpose and/or your writings from any one of the previous career analysis self-search exercises. The group should examine in turn each member's resume and those analysis notes which they are comfortable sharing.

Step 2:   Look over and discuss each other's writings. The quest is to identify all the significant clues revealed in each person's record and to discuss them with each other. It is not unlike detective work. A clue here and there detected by others in these discussions will reveal to you many more worklife options that you can identify working alone.

Step 3:   Now is the time for brainstorming. Each group member should seek to formulate career action steps for the others. Try a variety of configurations—rearrange the significant clues for each person several times. Challenge each group member to recommend what nature of job content or employment environment matches the data.

Step 4:   If appealing worklife opportunities do not emerge, then approach this exercise from a different direction. Group members should each write a recruitment advertisement for the kind of job tasks they believe they would enjoy. This forces each person to think in terms of preferred tasks to be performed and, in turn, the skills required to carry them out well and enjoyably.

Step 5:   The group should be asked to verify whether they would recruit each person for the position which has been described.

114
___

*Career
Analysis
and Life
Management
Planning*

Group work can be invaluable. It is an opportunity to talk through your viewpoints in a nonthreatening situation. It can motivate you to put more effort into the private time you allocate to career analysis and life management planning. An element of friendly competition often develops between members. This can help everyone to strive to be thorough and conscientious in their analysis.

Also, other people can identify values in you where you may have blind spots to characteristics of your personality, behavior and talents which should be taken into account. As you consider the comments of others whose opinion you respect, you are also able to view your perceived constraints in a different way.

A growing feeling of comradeship among self-help groups is very important. It is a lonely task to work out by yourself what you really want. The group setting promotes positive interaction and unity among members because of a shared purpose. Strong feelings of mutual help are generated which facilitate the process of analysis and development of realistic worklife options.

Occupational analysis

Gathering information about what is really required in terms of skills, capabilities and environmental conditions to effectively carry out the tasks of any job, is a skill in itself. Conduct the following analysis by working in groups of three people, each taking the turn of interviewer, interviewee and silent observer.

One person interviews another about what is actually done in their current job. Be prepared to explore the answers you get and ask for examples, situations or incidents. The interviewer's task is to find out what skills, training and knowledge are essential. The observer makes notes about both people's behavior, lists comments for feedback about the manner in which the discussion was conducted and audits the data elicited for any omissions. The quest is to find out a lot more about what is involved and the skills necessary for performing the job effectively.

This career opportunity awareness exercise develops your ability in several important areas. First, it gives practice in analyzing jobs and identifying the essential skills required to perform them. Second, it helps you develop research techniques which will contribute to your ongoing career management activities. And, finally, this exercise helps you form conclusions about how you would feel carrying out the tasks of a different type of job.

What you need to find out

Research into the likely supply and demand factors in your current occupation or an alternative you are considering requires that you prepare a number of questions. A useful way is to label a blank page with each of the following and then write down the data you acquire.

- Alternative job titles for the occupation

- Personal qualities required

- Tasks to be performed

- Skills required for these tasks

- Possible employers

- Employment outlook and opportunities

- Educational prerequisites

- Experience prerequisites

- Work environment conditions and location(s)

- Earnings — current and potential

Talking to those who can provide this information also requires preparation. The following is a guide for your preparation prior to meetings with such people.

- ☐ Having identified my prospect, would the person prefer a discussion at a place other than their work premises?

- ☐ Have my skills been prepared in clear classifications so that they will take no longer than two minutes to state when brought into conversation?

- ☐ Have I prepared my labelled pages on which to record the information I obtain at this discussion?

- ☐ Have I prepared key questions to find out who has the authority to hire in the area of my interest and what are the customary selection methods?

- ☐ Have I a resume clearly marked as a DRAFT to take to the meeting, ensuring that I leave it with the person I interviewed?

- ☐ Have I remembered to prepare a thank-you note to mail the day following the discussion?

116

Career
Analysis
and Life
Management
Planning

▓ *If you experience difficulty* ▓
identifying people with whom to carry out
occupational research refer to my book,
How to Network & Select a Mentor
(*The Center for Worklife Counselling*).

Occupational research

Your preparation should also involve listing the questions necessary to obtain the information you want. You will find out the answers by a mixture of reading appropriate literature and conducting information interviews with people. You should develop and write down your own questions before commencing research. Here are some of the most likely to help you get started with your list:

Nature of work

What physical and mental skills does this occupation require? Is the work carried out alone or is it dependent on the work of others? What are all the likely tasks in this occupation?

Personal qualities

What are the minimum physical and health standards? What personal attributes are evident in those who succeed in this occupation?

Education prerequisites

What are the qualifications employers are seeking for this occupation? Do they vary from one industry to another? What are regarded as "essential" qualifications and what are "desired" qualifications? Is there evidence of employers hiring applicants without either essential or desired qualifications?

Experience prerequisites

Does there appear to be a minimum period of experience required? What exactly is meant by "previous experience"?

Work environment conditions

What do people already in the occupation say they like best and dislike most? Is relocation a likely necessity for promotion or other reasons?

Earnings

What are the most dependable information sources for average earnings in the occupation? Does the earnings level vary in different parts of the country or industry? How are salary adjustments made? By merit review? Award? Consumer Price Index? Or a combination of these? Does one earn more or less with advancing age?

Employment outlook

What factors affect the future of the industry, the security of the occupation? What is the promotion rate within the occupation? What type of selection system determines promotion or transfer? Can this occupation be obtained anywhere I wish to live? What are related occupations to which I might transfer after a while? Does this industry favor unionists in its employment practices? Are there professional journals, newsletters or guides I should read to learn more about current trends in this occupation?

We need to research thoroughly in order to make an informed judgement about job content choice, career and potential employer.

118

*Career
Analysis
and Life
Management
Planning*

Reality test audit

Your quest for information is not complete until you can honestly answer "yes" to all the following questions:

- Do you actually know as much about the alternative occupation(s) you are considering as is expected of someone at your job level?

- Do you have a thorough perception of the present trends, the future outlook and the history which have a bearing on these?

- Are you now familiar with most of the major employers of the types of work activities you now know are most appropriate for you?

- What size, where do they operate, what is their current reputation, what appear to be their future plans? What appears to be the best way to approach these employers for a job?

- Have you learnt enough about the alternative occupations and related employers to be able to lead a conversation with intelligent questions and demonstrate the thoroughness of your research in the process? Are these questions written down and have they been reviewed by a person you respect?

The breadth and depth of the information you can obtain depends very much on you and the care you exercise in asking clearly for the information you want. These considerations may sound obvious but your future worklife satisfaction may depend on them. Don't take a casual or rushed pace through the reality testing phase. There is too much at stake to treat it other than thoroughly.

Career transition strategy

When you have determined the nature of job content, employment environment type and lifestyle implications and carried out the related occupational research, you should evaluate how you could achieve the transition. Check you have the answers to the following. If not, more research is required.

- Can you achieve the proposed transition with your current employer?

- Do you need additional training to improve your credentials for it? What nature of training? Where can it be obtained?

- What is regarded by other informed people as the most effective job search strategy for your target?

- What type of resume is applicable to increasing your likelihood of success in influencing relevant employment decision makers? Chronological? Functional? Portfolio? Curriculum Vitae? (For more information about resumes, consult *The Damn Good Resume Guide* by Yana Parker or *The Overnight Resume* by Donald Asher, both published by Ten Speed Press.)

8-DECISION LEARNING

Self-confidence about choosing the direction of your career comes from learning more about who you really are and what you want. This confidence can only be sustained by genuine feelings of achievement and implementing decisions you make in a desired career direction. You need to work continually at maintaining self-confidence during your career transition.

A good way of doing this is to decide each week what confidence building activity is to be your focus. Test this out right away. Make a commitment now to do something. Write down one or more action plans you believe you can realistically achieve in the next seven days. Review them at the end of this period and indulge in the new feeling of well-being their accomplishment has stimulated.

Decision-making courage

The past is what we build on, not despair about. Think about decisions you have made in the past; decisions which were considered at length before you made them and those you acted upon quickly. Recollect how you felt: (a) at the time; and (b) later when the outcomes of your decisions were clear. Record what happened when you:

- expressed an unpopular opinion firmly in the face of considerable opposition;

- did what felt right to you against the advice of others;

- understood training or a course of study in a subject totally new and different from your education and experience background;

- did something no one expected you to do;

- demonstrated by your actions that you could influence the direction of your life significantly;

- journeyed to a new place purely to experience excitement, curiosity and, perhaps, some danger;

- spent money on something which had an immediate payoff rather than debating whether it was practical.

Do you detect any similarities in the ways you made these decisions and your current approach to worklife decision making?

I would like to stop...

Procrastinating

Smoking

I would like to start when all I do is stop.

I would like to get off the treadmill,
   job, no job, no girl, job, no job, no girl.

I would like to stop the elevator and start using
   the stairs.

Recent counselling client

122

*Career
Analysis
and Life
Management
Planning*

The next 24 hours

Finding the self-confidence and energy to sustain yourself through the long process of career analysis and life management planning can come from genuine feelings of achievement. All of us, whatever our background, have accomplished worthwhile things and will continue to do so despite various obstacles.

Renew your energy by testing this out over the next twenty-four hours. Decide now to accomplish something important to you by this time tomorrow. Write down your commitment and what has to be done to realize it. Select an objective which is possible to achieve but will demand some special effort on your part to bring about its attainment. Remember the objective is to be important to you — not anybody else. Tomorrow evening review what happened. Think of the task or series of tasks you carried out towards this commitment. While reviewing what you have done, ponder your feelings. You are likely to feel good about your progress. Already your self-confidence has received an important boost.

Continue to practice setting one objective — a commitment — for each day over the next five days and put aside just half an hour every twenty-four hours to examine what occurred and how you feel about the events. The capacity to manage your career direction does not come automatically. It must be learned and practiced.

You are likely to find that you have improved your ability to decide on goals, set realistic objectives and schedules and identify resources required to help you succeed. This skills building should be practiced before you proceed to establish the longer-range objectives for your career and life management along the lines recommended in the following pages.

Work environment analysis

This exercise requires that you evaluate and decide about what sort of work situations appeal to you.

Look back over your career and think about the work environments you have experienced. Write down your answers to the following:

- Are you interested in large, small or medium-sized organizations in your next career action step?

- Are you interested in the consumer products, service, industrial products or human care industry sector?

- What appeals to you—light or heavy industry? service or white collar? self-employment? consultancy?

- What types of business or public sector organization that you know of excite or repel you?

- Do you need to work with a small team? on your own? with many people?

- So you want to command the work activity of others or influence people on a lateral relationship basis?

- What sort of reward system appeals to you: salary? payment on results? a mixture? status symbols? cars? profit-sharing? bonus? piece-work? hourly rate? List the components of your desired remuneration (pay method and employment benefits).

- Where would you like to work geographically?

- Where would you like to live geographically?

- What sort of pressures do you need on you to perform work activity at your best?

- How long do you want to stay in your next job? Is it a step to something else? What?

Employment environment conditions

It is a fact that once dislikes have been clearly identified, ways to avoid them come readily. If you know what's wrong, then you can decide what's right for you!

This exercise will contribute to screening out those occupations and employer types which will neither suit you nor increase your work satisfaction.

Your past employment experiences have been affected by many aspects of your employment environment. In fact, certain of these aspects would have prevented you from accomplishing some achievements of which you believed you were capable. In this quest for a more fulfilling worklife it's logical to identify those aspects which either discourage you or stimulate you to carry out job tasks better.

Write down all the factors within past employment environments you have disliked. Then, on a separate sheet of paper, write down those factors which you feel would enable you to work really well. Consider such things as the style of supervision you prefer; ground floor or window view work location; dealing with the public or working alone.

Here are several thought prompters to help you get under way with this decision learning exercise:

- How important is evidence to others of the status of your positions? Be very honest here. Consider size of office, desk, positioning, own telephone extension, etc.

- What business ethics matter to you?

- Under what styles of supervision do you work best — both from the aspect of your productivity and your happiness?

Your worklife expectations

People no longer believe that toil and self-denial eventually bring rewards or that accumulating material possessions gives life meaning. Instead, today's new achievers seek intangibles in the workplace, such as self-development, creativity, participation, freedom and a sense of wholeness and commitment.

P. Pascarella

To what extent does this statement reflect your views and expectations of worklife? Considering what you have written in response to

124

Career
Analysis
and Life
Management
Planning

this question, how would you rate your current employment environment as a workplace within which your expectations can be achieved?

Your values

In the course of carrying out our work our values are rarely the subject of introspection. Our worklife is often too fast for that. We choose, decide, make judgments and take action without conscious reference to them. But at the core of ourselves our values exist: they determine what we like and dislike, agree with or reject, judge as right or wrong. Where our values are in conflict with the content of our job or the nature of our employment environment, worklife satisfaction is not possible. By identifying our values we open up the possibility of choosing other ways of fulfilling our true self.

There are many ways in which you can determine your values. The following is just one of them. It is short and you may wish to extend the list before you make the choices this exercise asks you to make and record.

- Money

- Helping others

- Putting my lifestyle ahead of my job

- Continuing to learn

- Achieving a position of considerable influence over others

- Reaching my creative potential

- Living where I want to live

- _____

- _____

Write about five very good experiences and include specific information such as when, where and who else was involved. Then the five worst. Consider each experience you have described and write down what it is about the experience that you are valuing when you think about what occurred.

The five values most important to me deduced from these two exercises are:

1. _____

2. _____

3. _____

4. _____

5. _____

> ### *Does my proposed career action step fit comfortably with the values I hold important for my self-respect and sense of responsibility for those for whom I care?*

126

*Career
Analysis
and Life
Management
Planning*

Deciding where you want to work

Answer the following:

- Do I want to work for the public service, manufacturing or service industry, college education institution, an association, a union, myself (self-employment) or what?

- Do I want to work for a large established organization or a small one, where the going could be hectic but exciting?

- Do I want to join an organization with really difficult problems or one which appears to be safe and is likely to survive economic recessions?

- What time do I really want to get home at the end of my working day?

- What kinds of job/career pressures am I willing to work with and capable of — mentally and physically?

- What kinds of people do I want to work with? students, under-privileged, handicapped, elderly, professional, artistic, etc?

- What pay level do I need: (a) to meet basic expenses; and (b) to feel I'm enjoying life? What pay level do I need in three years' time?

- Do I want to work in a large city or small town? in which country? in what sort of climate?

- Have I discussed all these issues with my partner?

From a thorough review of the responses you have recorded to these questions, what conclusion can you make abut the most suitably sized organization for you? number of employees? local, nationwide, transnational, small business? Write down your views.

> *If you find it difficult to identify a clear pattern from a review of all your work to date and hence a desirable career path direction, seek an experienced counsellor. It's likely that the same counsellor can help with the identification of preferred occupation and the matching of your preference(s) with actual job availabilities.*

Objective setting

Copy the following Objective Setting Chart onto a pad of paper.

Step 1: List your new series of career objectives. Follow this by recording how you can attain these objectives.

Step 2: Identify and record what resources would help their achievement — people, information, new qualifications, etc.

Step 3: List what appear to be the obstacles which you need to overcome in order to reach you objectives — lack of time, money, promotion, transfer, etc.

The action of recording your objectives in this way will enable you to pinpoint any important issue which needs to be resolved. For example:

- Your overall plan may be unrealistic.

- You may need to do more fact gathering.

- You may need to change your order of priority.

- You could benefit from showing the data to other carefully selected people for their comment.

Objective Setting Chart

Career Objective	Order of Importance	Date to be Achieved	Method	Resources Required	Apparent Obstacles	Possible Solutions

Life planning

Your career planning should not be separated from life management planning. If you start towards your new worklife goals without preparing a life management plan, something will quickly go wrong. Conflicts will grow within yourself and between you and your loved one.

Here is a very important exercise to help you examine both areas and integrate the goals. This will increase your chances of inner well-being and clarify your next moves in both your career and personal life.

Step 1:   Take two sheets of paper and label one "What do I want to achieve in my career?" and the other "What do I want to achieve for personal — not work-related — fulfillment?"

Step 2:   List several objectives under each heading. Each should be your ideal but tempered by a realistic assessment of the likelihood that you will accomplish it. You will need at least eight objectives on each page. Don't write down more than twenty, otherwise you will have a problem deciding on their order of priority and establishing a clear realistic plan for their attainment.

Step 3:   Now, differentiate the importance of each objective by assessing them on a scale like this:

Ranking   Value

4-   of critical importance to me

3-   of considerable importance to me

2-   of moderate importance to me

1-   important, but not to the same degree as any of the others

Step 4:   On a third sheet arrange the objectives in order of your numerical rankings, i.e. put the 4s together, then the 3s, and so on, from the data you recorded on the first page. "What do I want to achieve in my career?" Do the same from the second page, "What do I want to achieve for personal — not work-related — fulfillment?"

Step 5:   At this stage concern yourself just with the 4s and 3s.

For each objective, write your answers to the following questions:

- What factors will affect my ability to achieve this?

- What hurdles, if any, need to be overcome?

- What might happen if I don't achieve this objective? How serious would this really be to me?

Step 6:   Analyze the 2s and 1s in the same way.

Step 7:   Now select from your list of objectives a few for detailed planning — the steps necessary, time schedule desired, resources you may need (money, education, help from others, etc.) — and proceed to draw up an action plan. Take a break, then return to complete the planning for the remaining objectives.

Step 8:   The value of this exercise is considerably extended if you share the data you have recorded with other people. In a group setting, read one another's reports. Discuss the contents and why certain decisions were made. You will find similar themes, yet each will have arrived at their conclusions differently.

Contribute by helping each other audit data for:

- clarity of objectives;

- thoroughness;

- appraisal of hurdles to overcome;

- identification of resources to be found.

130

*Career
Analysis
and Life
Management
Planning*

Sharing your ideas with others helps clarify your own values and priorities. Nevertheless, the degree to which you share your personal thoughts with others is an important factor. There is no value in making yourself uncomfortable by sharing confidences of an intimate nature.

Whether you carried out this exercise alone or with other people, you are likely to have changed the priorities of your objectives as you observed how some could not be achieved without risking the achievement of others.

This complex, but valuable, exercise should result in a realistic set of career and life management plans with which you are satisfied. You will probably also have a considerable feeling of accomplishment — very few people ever complete such a detailed and thoughtful assessment of where they are going in life.

*Deciding on a new career direction
does not mean giving up what we are.
It means expanding what we are.*

Support group testing

Here is a further opportunity to use others as resources to test the reality of your goal and check whether all other alternatives have been considered.

Form a group of no less than three — each preferably from a different occupation or industry.

Your task as a group is to:

- select one or more real career goal problem(s); each problem must be one with which a group member is encountering difficulty in believing can be accomplished;

- discuss the ways in which the problem can be resolved, what hurdles have to be overcome, what resources can be used both within and outside their employment which would assist its attainment;

- discuss how much employment security each person honestly needs to enjoy living;

- discuss how much each person is prepared to forego and/or risk —in terms of time, money, personal relationships — to reach their goals;

- make a concluding presentation to the others and receive critical appraisal and constructive comment.

▨ *Decision learning is about* ▨
taking risks which research has
shown are worth taking.

Career path decision making

Consider the decision you need to make. It is likely to be between two or more career direction alternatives.

Step 1: For each alternative write down a list of as many outcomes as you can think of. Some will be negative and others positive in nature.

Step 2: Assign to each outcome on your list a number, a value, from -10 to +10. When values approach 0 the outcome is of little or low importance in relation to others on your list. The negative outcomes should be recorded as a minus, that is, -10 to -1.

Step 3:   For each outcome listed, evaluate the probability that
           it will happen. For example, 0 is that the outcome will
           definitely not occur. 10 is that it definitely will occur. 5
           indicates a fifty-fifty chance that it will occur. Write
           these figures in the second column.

Step 4:   Multiply the value of each outcome by the probability
           of it occurring. Write these answers in the third column.
           Add up this column.

Repeat this procedure for each of the other alternatives.

Step 5:   The alternative with the highest expected value is a guide
           to the most appropriate option for you to take.

132

*Career
Analysis
and Life
Management
Planning*

From my decision learning what have I selected?
Moving up — promotion?
Moving sideways — lateral job change?
Moving out — resigning?
Moving down — deliberately seeking demotion?
Consolidating — enriching current job?

9- TRANSITION TRAINING

T his chapter requires the same self-honesty you have applied so far in completing the self-search and life planning exercises. It is, in fact, the testing point for taking charge of the management of your own career. Don't avoid answering. Don't "cheat a little." It's your life under consideration.

Worklife change analysis

For the purposes of preparing for your career action steps towards your new goals, think back over your past worklife changes. Think about and jot down:

- the easiest change you have made in: (a) job content; (b) employment environment; and (c) lifestyle;
- the most difficult;
- the risks you have taken to further your career;
- what made one easier/more difficult than another;
- what factors were involved in getting into job situations you have enjoyed.

Reflect upon and record the experiences you have had and the resources you are now able to bring to the worklife transitions you have planned and will make soon. What are your strengths? What strategies can you further develop? What resources will you need to make the changes you want? What skills training do you need to reduce the risk of not fulfilling your plans?

Career charting

Using the Planning Form and Monitor Chart which follow, produce career charts for your future worklife.

Planning Form

Today's date: _____		
One of my goals is to: _____		
_____		

Actions necessary to achieve the goal	Whose help do I need?	Target date to complete action

Goal to be achieved by: _____

_____

Step 1: At the top of the Planning Form enter today's date and a description of your goal.

Step 2: Think through all the actions you need to take to move towards and reach each goal. List them.

Step 3: Alongside each action, enter a date by which you can reasonably expect that it will be complete. Remember not to set yourself the impossible, nor to make your deadlines so far ahead that progress will feel unduly slow.

Step 4: Select other people you will need to assist your journey to each goal. Enter their names in the second column. Soon you must contact them to explain what you are doing and to ask for their help.

Step 5: Enter the date by which you aim to have completed all the necessary actions and so to have reached each goal.

■ **When we know what we want,** ■
why we merit it and what is necessary to
achieve it, worklife can be regarded more
positively as a source of rewards and
enrichment of our journey through life.
Our preparation for the rest of worklife
must be thorough and complete.

Step 6: When you have completed your Planning Form for each goal, summarize them on the Monitor Chart. This will enable you to record your progress and see your whole program at a glance.

Step 7: Recheck the goals, actions and schedules you have selected for yourself by talking them over with a friend who will be reasonably objective about them.

Monitor Chart

Goals	Action target dates	Completion date for goal
1_____ _____ _____	1 2 3	
2_____ _____ _____	1 2 3	
3_____ _____ _____	1 2 3	
4_____ _____ _____	1 2 3	

136

*Career
Analysis
and Life
Management
Planning*

Audit Your Career Transition Preparation

Circle the number you consider applies to you

Scale: 1 - strongly agree   4 - disagree
         2 - agree   5 - strongly disagree
         3 - maybe, not certain

I can now list the most important personal factors that will affect my career over the next three years.	1 2 3 4 5
I can now list at least four critical employment environment factors that will influence my career progress with my current employer.	1 2 3 4 5
I now know at least two realistic career action steps for me with my current employer.	1 2 3 4 5
I now know which responsibilities are mine and which are my employer's concerning the development of my career.	1 2 3 4 5
I have researched and committed to the necessary training courses and development experiences to prepare for my next career action step.	1 2 3 4 5
I now know how to identify an appropriate mentor and secure their assistance.	1 2 3 4 5
I have recorded an unambiguous set of career goals and a schedule for achieving each stage towards them.	1 2 3 4 5
I am clear on the essential requirements and the desirable features in my next career move.	1 2 3 4 5
I know the reasons for my past career move choices.	1 2 3 4 5
I have sorted out my key strengths and accomplishments in terms of my career to date.	1 2 3 4 5
I now know how to measure the value of a job to my overall career before taking it.	1 2 3 4 5

Add the numbers you have circled for your total score. If your total score is more than 24, you need to redo some of the preceding exercises.

Commitment Checklist

Yes / No

Have I now carried out the most thorough self-analysis and personal goal setting I have ever done? ☐ ☐

Have I identified my strongest skills and interests? Are they those I have used best and enjoyed most? ☐ ☐

Have I identified different ways in which these skills and interests can be used? For instance, public speaking, lecturing, selling, acting, etc. ☐ ☐

Have I identified the most appropriate occupation for my unique set of skills and capabilities? ☐ ☐

Have I researched what it really entails, where it is available and the employers with whom it exists? ☐ ☐

Do I know the supply and demand features of the occupation in the short-term future? ☐ ☐

If additional retraining is involved, do I know where tuition is available? which study pattern is most appropriate for my needs? enrollment procedure? ☐ ☐

Have I developed and written down a career chart strategy and timetable? Does it fit into my new total lifestyle plan? ☐ ☐

Do I know now what I want to achieve in life — not just in work activity? ☐ ☐

Does the analysis of my self-search data show that my work is not the issue but rather, it is the nature or lack of other activities in my life? ☐ ☐

What are my particular values? Have I assessed them in relation to status, popularity, recognition, a sense of belonging, power, money, achievement, relationships with others, those dependent on me? ☐ ☐

Has expanding my self-knowledge increased my personal energy to a level sufficient to succeed? ☐ ☐

Have I allocated the time within which I want to make changes? for example, when the youngest child leaves school, before I'm forty, when the second mortgage is paid off. ☐ ☐

Have I obtained from a competent person a true financial appraisal of my assets and liabilities? ☐ ☐

Have I discussed all of the above with my partner, best friend or a reliable, competent counsellor? ☐ ☐

Final check

You have assembled and analyzed a vast amount of information; you have researched and selected occupational alternatives and identified potential employers. It has been a long, taxing effort — one you can feel proud of and be grateful for in the years ahead. But a note of caution! It's a world of continual change. Personal circumstances, education requirements, supply and demand conditions in the employment market, and the overall economy of the country can all produce crises which may threaten the successful conclusion of your quest. So check your personal data and research information regularly, recheck some of your sources of information, make sure your objective is still realistically obtainable. If events have made it impractical to continue, all is not necessarily lost and the search should not be abandoned.

138

*Career
Analysis
and Life
Management
Planning*

Your original analysis produced many transferable skills and interests. It was only a later stage of your work which applied a particular occupational label or job title. Review your original analysis again. There will be alternative occupations which could appeal to you just as strongly and your campaign can begin again with renewed vigor. This time the research will take less time as you already known what sources are likely to be of most help —both people and printed materials.

Is resignation necessary?

You have researched opportunities for transfer to tasks more suited to your skills, capabilities and interests in your current employment. Your employer has a vested interest in retaining you for many reasons. The knowledge you have about the organization, its services, products, procedures and style are costly to impart to a new employee, in addition to the recruitment expenses of the search for another person if you should leave.

You should think very carefully before resigning. A carefully prepared presentation to people with the authority to arrange job content changes, transfers or promotions should be considered. They will expect you to have prepared a sound case for your request. The higher the people within the organization with whom you discuss your situation, the more authority exists to change tasks within jobs, create new positions or arrange transfers. The essential components of your strategy for change within your current job include selecting who to talk to, seeking a time when privacy can be assured and thoroughly rehearsing the presentation of your request.

In the process of discussing your career with them you may learn more about alternative opportunities within the organization than you knew before. You may secure a commitment to facilitating your reassignment and thus avoid the strain and hazards of a search for a different employer.

Do complete the following checklist before you consider resigning, as your answers may reveal that this is not the most appropriate action for you to take. Have you:

- found out what your boss regards as good performance? It may differ from your current opinion.

- mastered your job as quickly as possible and passed on your knowledge to another person? In this way, lack of suitable replacement will not stop your promotional or transfer chances.

- learned to like yourself as a unique human being? There is no need for you to wait in the wings. You need to move yourself into the spotlight so others can see, respect and admire you.

- stepped outside the confines of your job description, but made sure your actions are regarded as initiative, rather than rule breaking?

- expanding opportunities for those in power to learn more about you by achieving success in activities outside work, such as community service organizations and/or personal development studies?

- identified a mentor in a senior position where you work from whom to seek career advice, and returned the favor with loyalty and respect?

- suggested thoroughly prepared remedies — not criticisms — for problems within your employment environment?

- developed your skills in interpersonal relationships? accepted the fact that office politics exist? reexamined your personal values, so that when faced with ethical dilemmas at work, you know what to do without procrastinating?

- recognized that ability alone will not advance your career? Persistence, hard work and being seen as personally ambitious—but an effective team member—are all important attributes to cultivate.

- smile a lot? Managers notice and favor people with happy but conscientious dispositions. The glum people are often regarded as too risky to move to higher level positions.

- ensured you have a good variety of interests outside your worklife career to alleviate the negative aspects of stress?

- practices self-nomination? Don't wait to be offered job content change, promotion or transfer. Let it be known what you want and demonstrate how you qualify for it.

140

*Career
Analysis
and Life
Management
Planning*

Test Your Job-Seeking Skills

Circle the number you consider applies to you

Scale: 1 - strongly agree   4 - disagree

         2 - agree   5 - strongly disagree

         3 - maybe, not certain

I know what skills I can offer employers.	1 2 3 4 5
I know what skills employers most seek in my target occupation.	1 2 3 4 5
I have a copy of the membership directory of the association of my target occupation to use for networking purposes.	1 2 3 4 5
I know how to research different recruitment agencies, employers and organizations in a public library and career reference centers.	1 2 3 4 5
I can explain convincingly to interviewers what I did well for my last employer.	1 2 3 4 5
I can give three good reasons why an employer should hire me.	1 2 3 4 5

I can secure the support of my family and friends
for making a job or career change.   1 2 3 4 5

I can allocate ten to fifteen hours each week to
conduct a job search if need be.   1 2 3 4 5

I can write different types of resumes, job search
letters and follow-up letters.   1 2 3 4 5

I can distribute resumes and letters to the ten
most relevant recruitment consultancies and
employment agencies.   1 2 3 4 5

I can list my major worklife accomplishments
in ways in which the results are clear and
quantifiable.   1 2 3 4 5

I can identify no less than ten employers with
whom I want to obtain interviews.   1 2 3 4 5

I have three carefully prepared questions for
when interviewers ask me: "Any questions?"   1 2 3 4 5

I can develop a job vacancy referral network to
help me.   1 2 3 4 5

I know how to prospect for job leads where none
are advertised.   1 2 3 4 5

I can use the telephone to "cold call" and get
interviews.   1 2 3 4 5

I can plan and implement an effective direct-mail
job search of unsolicited inquiries to at least
thirty employers.   1 2 3 4 5

Add the numbers you have circled for a total score. If you
score is more than 40 points, you need to work more on
developing your job-seeking skills. Referring to two other
books I have written will help you — *Your Job Search
Organizer* (Pitman Publishing) and *Win That Job!* (The Center
for Worklife Counselling).

Career transition checklist

Yes / No

- *I have thought about and defined the type of work-lifestyle I want and merit.* ☐ ☐

- *I have identified personality characteristics that should be considered in selecting my next boss.* ☐ ☐

- *I know my feelings about the work environment setting I would like.* ☐ ☐

- *I have identified potential employers relevant to my career path choice.* ☐ ☐

- *I have talked to two or more people already in the occupation I am targeting.* ☐ ☐

- *I have identified the relevant actual job titles I am considering.* ☐ ☐

- *I have identified additional skills-building needs I should fulfill in my next job.* ☐ ☐

- *I have obtained references from past employers.* ☐ ☐

- *I have prepared a good resume and practiced writing cover letters.* ☐ ☐

- *I have researched data about at least four possible employers.* ☐ ☐

- *I have an understanding of the different approaches used to obtain interviews.* ☐ ☐

- *I know what I want and how to go after it.* ☐ ☐

- *I have achievable alternatives in mind if unable initially to get my first choice.* ☐ ☐

- *I have talked over my career transition goals with the significant others in my life.* ☐ ☐

▓ 10-PROTECTING YOUR ▓ ACHIEVEMENT

Y ou are likely to have implemented successfully several career actions as a result of your hard work in the preceding chapters. But just because you have been successful does not mean that management of your career is completed. Sustaining worklife satisfaction is, in many employment environments, even more difficult than finding it. Consequently, you must pay attention to how to sustain and protect it, and grow further in your worklife.

Sustaining career satisfaction consists of several phases. These cover understanding the nature of the world of work, analyzing the communication networks where you work, growing in your mastery of your job and building cooperation from those with whom you work.

Office politics

If I reviewed all the conversations with clients of my worklife counselling practice over the last eleven years, there is one feature of life at work which crops us repeatedly — office politics. This seems to be the aspect of work with which people have the most difficulty.

Political behavior at work is a proudly acknowledged skill when our careers are advancing satisfactorily, but is denigrated when we suffer a setback as a consequence of it. A significant number of my clients initially express annoyance and frustration when they are the victims of adverse events. Yet if we reflect for a moment that career management is as much about our ability to handle interactions with other people as about choosing the right employer at the right time, then the existence of office politics seems normal and rational.

There is nothing mysterious about office politics. It is simply another phrase for interpersonal relationships. The trouble is our high school or college careers advisers often failed to mention its existence and provided little or no training in how to manage the process. Finding the optimum fit between our career preparation and personal goals was their main message. Little attention was paid to the realities of work or the fact that choice of occupation and employer is a lifelong process of decision making. I have no hesitation in sharing that my counselling work is as much about helping people adjust to the social system of employment life as helping clients develop and choose between career and life management alternatives.

We have explored in this book how our work satisfaction depends on the extent to which we find adequate outlets for our abilities, interests, personality and values as each of these changes throughout adulthood. It depends on finding the type of work and way of life in which we can behave in a role we find congenial and consider appropriate for our uniqueness. As we role-play, so do others, but often with different sets of motivations. A collision course is inevitable if we do not learn how to steer our career path skillfully. The process of managing our careers is essentially that of developing what we want and deciding what is realistic. This, however, cannot occur in isolation from other people unless we are the only person on the payroll.

Interpersonal relationships

Whenever people gather together politics are created and this is very much in evidence in employment environments. Unfortunately, many people are either insensitive to the political behavior of fellow employees or seek ways in which they can avoid participating, often to the detriment of their careers.

Politics at work is about power and interpersonal relationships.

Where two or more people focus on problems in order to make and implement decisions, coalitions are formed. Rarely do these coalitions remain stable. The nature of work activity, other than lighthouse keeping, demands that people interact with each other. The social forces that are consequently involved in these interactions form the kernel of worklife politics. The essence of the political contract between two or more people is: "I'll support your efforts if you'll support mine." This needs to be achieved without creating antagonism. It's not necessary to be friendly with everyone, but you should at least seek neutrality, not outright hostility, if support cannot be secured from relevant quarters.

144

*Career
Analysis
and Life
Management
Planning*

The alert, career-conscious person acknowledges the existence of office politics and sets out to study the nature of interpersonal relationships. By acquiring an understanding of why people behave the way they do, you are better able to adjust your behavior in order to influence events to favor your career rather than jeopardize it. Those who do not give attention to increasing their skills in interpersonal relationships may have considerable difficulty sustaining and increasing their worklife satisfaction.

Hard work and a virtuous image alone do not advance careers. Participation in political behavior is risky but necessary. Beverly L. Kaye, in her impressive book, *Up is Not the Only Way to Go* (Prentice-Hall), suggests clear approaches to thinking and acting politically. She writes that such thinking may involve:

- Visibility: making sure that accomplishments become well-known, by sending memos, circulating reports, making presentations at meetings.

- Attention: getting the ear of people who are in positions of influence and power.

- Association: forming friendships and networks with valuable contact people at lunches, seminars, conferences.

- Information: gathering inside information from such diverse sources as secretaries, auditors, managers.

- Aspirations: making career advancement ambitions known to those who can assist.

- Demonstration: finding opportunities to demonstrate abilities by volunteering for committee assignments, special projects and oral presentations.

Beverly Kaye warns that to ignore office politics is a myopic view which can hinder your progress at work. "Only by recognizing, studying and understanding the internal political system can you take advantage of the opportunities it affords." Determined career strategists learn where to voice their ideas so that they are implemented and won't wither and die. They know when it is possible to let someone else move on their behalf. They know that changes in an organization rarely occur because of their actions alone. Change requires the support of several people who feel that the change might bring some good for them as well.

Personality types

It would be a false assumption to regard only the dominant and strongly voiced people as being capable of skillful career protection. The quietly motivated, achievement-oriented person who cares less for power than the attainment of self-set goals can be just as adept in its usage. And the quickly dismissed "office friendly" — the person with an obvious desire to be liked by all — is frequently more adept than the former two personality types at surviving well at work.

Skill at office politics is not limited to personality type but more to those astute employees who acknowledge it as a fact of life and study how to manage their fate, not surrender to it.

Let's examine briefly two recurring situations where there is a right way and a wrong way to handle the political aspects.

The incompetent supervisor

146

*Career
Analysis
and Life
Management
Planning*

Being assigned to a supervisor who is not a competent performer of their own job tasks can be very frustrating. There is a danger that if your supervisor does not have high standards you may adjust yours downwards in order not to disturb your relationship with that person.

Alternatively you may decide to resign, when staying with the employer could be the better course to follow, provided that you assess your position carefully and adopt a suitable course of action.

It is easier to show those in higher, more powerful positions your personal competence, ambition and enthusiasm when you are supervised by an incompetent supervisor.

A politically wrong move would be to behave disloyally to take underhand actions like routing your work around your boss to higher levels. Experience has taught me that an incompetent supervisor is well-known to others higher in the organization. They take care to pay special attention to that unit or department in order to protect their reputation and business interests. In such a situation you can be very visible. To perform better than others in a demoralized department requires only your determination to do so. It's a precious career management sign for you to get in charge of your destiny and excel. Your reward should not be long in arriving.

Criteria for promotion

It is a rare employment environment that will advance your cause without your own attempts to discover the criteria for promotion. Sharp career strategists look for problems in the organization to which they might contribute solutions; they identify and cultivate the most useful people; they seek their counsel. A self-defeating course of action would be to complain to coworkers that your talents are being ignored. Inevitably, news of your views will travel and, at some stage, be regarded negatively rather than acted upon positively.

To manage your career well, you must be appropriately active — not simply reactive — to what others decide or choose for you. Find time to probe diplomatically. The contents of your job description are not engraved in stone. If you work solely to its contents you will miss important clues for enriching your worklife situation. Those who do search for clues and find them are rewarded for their initiative.

Happiness at work

As most of us have to spend many hours a day earning a living, it's worth pausing to focus on ways of making this time more enjoyable. Work as a source of happiness doesn't necessarily mean doing what we like, but liking what we do. Maintaining interest each day, taking pride in working well and being consistently enthusiastic may mean managing our own attitude towards work. It won't help to dwell on the prospect of doing the same things day in, day out, for the next twenty or thirty years. Managing attitudes towards work is as important to the would-be career path changer as to the people who are resolved to continue in their present occupation. Almost every job has aspects which are repetitive and undemanding. All work activity can be a source of depression rather than happiness if we allow it to be. To decide that we, as individuals, can make work enjoyable rather than depending solely on our employer's actions, is an important turning point in our quest for satisfaction from employment life.

Attitude management requires only a few steps. For example, take one day at a time and concentrate on the present moment in each day. Resolve that today is yours to enjoy at work. Don't dwell on tomorrow or next week or next month. Certainly, there are problems to solve, obstacles to overcome and anxiety-producing situations to experience. They will seem less formidable by looking at the activity you are engaged in now and resolving to do it as best you can. We do not like ourselves when we know that we are applying our minimum effort to our job tasks.

View work as being desirable. For example, working redirects your thoughts away from personal problems; it can prevent boredom — that demoralizing boredom which comes from little mental or physical activity (as so many of the unemployed experience); it is the source of the money that enables you to survive, to buy both the things you need in order to live and those that enrich your living — books, travel and entertainment.

While you are planning your next career action step, train yourself to do your current job well. Tell yourself it doesn't really matter if the job you do falls short of your objective. Regard it as a dress rehearsal for what you will eventually gain when the job breaks occur. Concentrate on the results of your day's work rather than the routine. Keep the challenge foremost in your thoughts and refuse to backtrack or give up.

When work for the day is completed, transfer your attention to other things. Without a hobby or other activity your leisure time can be dreary, allowing your thoughts to slip back to work problems. Community service, sports, researching a new area of learning, writing short stories or joining a special interest group are examples of activities which can be done outside working hours and which are marvelous therapy for improving your attitudes towards work.

Examining your attitude towards work can help clarify whether a change in occupation is really the answer to an improvement in your worklife.

148

*Career
Analysis
and Life
Management
Planning*

▧ *Congratulations!*

You've done it! You have:

- *identified clearly what kind of person you really are and determined what you want to do with your life;*
- *achieved this by discovering where you are today, how you got here and where you now want to go;*
- *researched, evaluated and decided how you will get there;*
- *collected appropriate information and planned what you will do when you arrive;*
- *worked out how to begin and see through your career transition journey.*

No one can say that you are postponing the rest of your life —particularly not you.

▓ BIBLIOGRAPHY ▓

Bolles, Richard Nelson. *What Color Is Your Parachute?* Ten Speed Press, Berkeley, California, 1991.

Calvert, R., Durkin, B., Grandi, E., Martin, K. *First Find Your Hilltop*, Hutchinson Business Books, London, 1990.

d'Apice, Mary. *Noon to Nightfall*, Collins Dove, Melbourne, 1989.

Lewis, S. and Cooper, C.L. *Career Couples*, Allen & Unwin, Sydney, 1990.

O'Collins, Gerald. *The Second Journey: Spiritual Awareness and the Mid-Life Crisis*, Dove Communications, Melbourne, 1979.

Potter, Beverly A. *Maverick Career Strategies: The Way of Rodin*, Amacom, New York, 1986.

Probert, Belinda. *Working Life*, McPhee Gribble, Melbourne, 1989.

Salmon, Phillida. *Living In Time: A New Look at Personal Development*, J.M. Dent & Sons, London, 1985.

Sinetar, Marsha. *Do What You Love, The Money Will Follow*, Dell Publishing, New York, 1987.

Smith, Shirley. *Set Yourself Free*, Transworld, 1990.

Stinson, Rod. *Job Prospects Australia*, Hobsons Press, Sydney, 1989.

Stoodley, Martha. *Information Interviewing: What it is and How to Use it in Your Career*, Garrett Park Press, Maryland, 1990.

Tulku, Tarthang. *Skillful Means*, Dharma Publishing, Berkeley, California, 1978.

Use Your Initiative: Enterprise Skills for the Future, Australian Government Publishing Service, Canberra, 1990.

ABOUT THE AUTHOR

P aul Stevens has thirty-three years' experience in career guidance and human resource development. He is a National Committee member of the Australian Association of Career Counsellors as well as the founder and director of The Center for Worklife Counselling, Sydney. In addition, Paul is a regular radio broadcaster on worklife issues and is frequently engaged by commercial, public sector and community service organizations to conduct career management training for employees and career counsellors. He was appointed as a representative for Australia to the editorial board of the *International Journal of Career Management* and was the recipient of the 1991 Resource Award from the Career Planning and Adult Development Network of California.

The author of twenty-four publications, including *The Australian Resume Guide, Win That Job!, Your Career Planner, Your Job Search Organizer* and the WORKLIFE Series, Paul is also the author, designer and publisher of a set of Career Development Resource Kits as well as the definitive text for career counsellors and trainers, *Career Transitions*. Paul has extended his work to include career support to members of religious orders and has been engaged as a government consultant, devising innovative measures which assist both employer and employee to cope with change.

▨ AN EXPLANATION ▨ —WORKLIFE

T he Center for Worklife Counselling often provokes comment about its name. The term "worklife" was chosen to reflect our continuing work in research, counselling, training and publishing material which relates to improving people's enjoyment from their employment activities and other aspects of their lives.

We do not accept the traditional view of career counselling, that is, to help people acquire satisfaction only from their working hours. We consider that occupational satisfaction can only occur when a person's total needs are included in the assessment of what is lacking and what needs to be done to increase inner well-being, improved relationships with others, and effective performance both at work and nonwork activities. Ours is a holistic approach — we try to consider all features of a person while maintaining respect for personal privacy by the use of nonthreatening inquiries into thoughts and circumstances.

Our publications reflect this philosophy.

from P.82   objectives from mid-teens

Self
✓ Success at team sports
  (Largely oriented, with short
bursts of enthusiasm for specifics eg.
Ford placement) — Recognition by others
✓ Take control — control over others
✓ Get into blue chip/prestige career
  Independence/self sufficiency vs. gregariousness
  Always progress at faster than
average rate X (one of pairs last few years
  eg: good Uni degree / A Levels X
? ✓ Find partner — of set shot ; fears are
                  V. happy now
✓ Escape to Oz — but what then?
✓ Balance life — fulfillment & enjoyment

      ✓ Better ; so much more to achieve
Develop extracurricular interests — happening sporadically
Find true goals for life / develop shorter-term perspective — need to continue self-
✓ Travel widely / experience / new things   into longer-range   aware

Others (Not listened to/
                      invited many)
✓ Grampy — live up to Grandpa's exped'
  (career-oriented) — no longer a fa
  ≥ a motivating memory (little book)
  School — Oakridge (rejected)
      — Exam results / good Uni degr.
      — Leadership / Example-setting
Fulfil potential
(V. little, if anything communicated at
    home)

      Skills used in pursuing objectives — High aptitude for all
                                        High enjoyment for all, off
Seizing opportunities (& seeking them out to an extent)   slightly less so for 'maturity' ones
Self-belief ; given pleasure to significant other as lover & friend   million 100 of childhood/naively
Selling self successfully / beating high calibre competition eg. UCL, U, Oz residency
Mature / Responsibility for self / Forward-looking & optimistic / Holistic approach to life
Honesty / Integrity / dynamically   Innovative   Zest for life
Pursuing tenaciously / when definitely want something (usually then comes
Empathy / recognising appropriate behaviour for different situations / Leaders   quietly
Judgement / Intellect / Pragmatic / Successfully balance academic/work with outsi
Consideration of others' positions (not nec₄ acted upon)   interests
Integrating self into a team ; overcome health obstacles ; enjoyed communal
From P. 83 — Achievements to date   successes as
                                                                 well as personal

Paul Paglioni contact & subsequent Ford placement at CRAC course

Getting myself around the world

Job offers from Fords & U

Smooth closure of Hackney esp. dealing w. other mgrs, neg'ns, driving outplacement
  obtaining genuine admiration from IGW

1st real job at George Hotel

R/ship w. D throughout closure & subsequent strength

Going thro' w. Oz residency applic'n

Outcome of Sydney visit & refocusing on importances

Solid 6 mnths work for good III₁

Other books from Ten Speed Press you may find helpful

WHAT COLOR IS YOUR PARACHUTE? by Richard N. Bolles

This classic in the career field is substantially revised and updated every year. In each new edition Bolles tries to offer the job seeker a better way to personalize their job search. Practical advice, step-by-step exercises, and a warm, human tone combine to make PARACHUTE essential for anyone looking for a new job or career change. The *New York Times* called PARACHUTE "the giant title in the field," and over five million job-hunters agree.

$14.95 paper, 480 pages

HOW TO CREATE A PICTURE OF YOUR IDEAL JOB OR NEXT CAREER by Richard N. Bolles

This workbook, taken from PARACHUTE, helps job-hunters identify the skills they most enjoy using, and the work setting which will be most satisfying. Covers long- and short-term planning, salary negotiation, and other important issues.

$4.95 paper, 64 pages

THE THREE BOXES OF LIFE And How to Get Out of Them by Richard N. Bolles

This practical yet creative book goes a step beyond PARACHUTE, to provide a wider view or transitions and a wonderful toolkit for self-assesment and integrated life/work planning. ". . . a rich and rewarding guidebook that provides literally hundreds of resources and opportunities for growth." — *Library Journal*

$14.95 paper, 480 pages

SWEATY PALMS by H. Anthony Medley

One of the most popular books ever on job interviewing, fully revised and updated for the 90s. Tells how to prepare for an interview, answer difficult or illegal questions, and leave a great impression. Special sections on dealing with discrimination or harassment.

$9.95 paper, 194 pages

THE DAMN GOOD RESUME GUIDE by Yana Parker

Our bestselling resume book, updated with 22 all-new functional-style resumes. Shows how to turn your resume into a vital self-marketing tool, not just a boring list of jobs. Sections on informational interviewing, targeting your resume to your job objective, and integrating work and nonwork experience.

$6.95 paper, 80 pages

Available from your local bookstore, or order direct from the publisher. Please include $2.50 shipping & handling for the first book, and 50 cents for each additional book. California residents include local sales tax. Write for our free catalog of over 400 books, posters, and tapes. For VISA or MASTERCARD call (800)841-BOOK.

Ten Speed Press   Box 7123   Berkeley, Ca 94707